IT Business

Partnerships

A FIELD GUIDE

IT Business

Partnerships

A FIELD GUIDE

*Paving the Way for
Business & Technology
Convergence*

Joseph Topinka

Foreword by John Sculley
Former Apple CEO

IT Business Partnerships: A Field Guide

Copyright © 2014 by Joseph Topinka

CIO Mentor Press

CIO
MENTOR
press

ISBN-13: 978-0-9893809-0-4
LCCN: 2013956352

Distributed by Itasca Books

Editing by Danielle Schweich Freudenthal
Cover Design by Jacqueline Meisel
Illustrations, *The Pains of Today*, *A Brighter Tomorrow* by Loraine Potter

Printed in the United States of America

To Bob and Clara Topinka,
the most influential leaders in my life.

Credits

Author
Joseph R. Topinka

Edited by
Danielle Schweich Freudenthal

Foreword by
John Sculley

Cover Design by
Jacqueline Meisel

Table of Contents

About the Author

In 2001, Joseph Topinka established CIO Mentor, LLC, a consultancy focused on helping mid-market companies leverage the power of technology to achieve profit-driven business results. With more than ten years of coaching and mentoring experience, Joe has helped numerous IT leaders and CIOs establish governance processes and IT Business Partnership programs in many companies. In 2013, Joe's achievements were recognized when he was named a CIO of the Year by Minneapolis/St. Paul Business Journal.

Joe is currently Chief Information Officer and VP of Multichannel Commerce for Red Wing Shoe Company, a privately held, US-based global manufacturer of performance footwear and garments. As a member of the executive management team, Joe contributes seasoned, broad-based perspectives and pragmatic, cost-effective IT strategies and solutions. Among his achievements, Joe drove a multimillion-dollar multichannel commerce initiative that transformed the Red Wing Shoe Company's go-to-market strategy in all worldwide markets.

Prior to joining Red Wing Shoe Company, Joe was CIO of RSM McGladrey, the fifth-largest accounting firm in the United States. Joe was responsible for the firm's IT strategy and operations. He served on the firm's senior leadership team and led numerous strategic initiatives, including the introduction of new platforms for the firm's audit and tax practices, implementing the firm's first IT governance business process; he also led the technology integration of newly acquired American Express Tax and Business Services.

In addition, Joe served as Chief Information Officer for BNY Clearing Services, a wholly-owned subsidiary of Bank of New York. His accomplishments include establishing the information technology function for BNY Clearing Services by creating business-oriented solutions for internal and external customers. He also developed and implemented an e-commerce strategy and executed one of the first web-based brokerage workstations in the industry.

Joe began his IT career at Metavante, Inc., (now FIS), a major financial services and software provider headquartered in Milwaukee. As a business unit manager, Joe was responsible for developing software solutions for commercial banks. His accomplishments include the creation of leading account analysis, profitability systems, and customer relationship management systems, which were market leaders in their category. Prior to this role, Joe was a software engineer.

Acknowledgments

I've held many positions during my more than 35-year career in IT, beginning as a software engineer writing software for financial institutions. Some of the software I created is still in use today, and I might have been happy to make a career as a developer. During that time, though, I was thrust into situations that revealed I also had a knack for understanding and motivating people. This fueled a strong, enduring interest in corporate strategy and an understanding of what makes businesses work. These skills developed concurrently during my career and eventually converged, helping me secure my first CIO role more than 15 years ago. I want to extend my thanks to those managers that recognized the leadership potential in me at the start of my career and to those that promoted me as my career progressed.

As it turns out, coaching and mentoring IT leaders has been one of the most rewarding aspects of my career. Frankly, I have learned more from these experiences than I have from just about anything else I have done. In sharing my successes and failures, the individuals I mentor have given me perspectives that help me perform better as a leader. Many of them encouraged me to share my stories so more people could benefit from our collective experiences.

My wife was inspirational and a never-ending source of encouragement, finally convincing me to take the plunge and write the book. The summer of 2012, we decided to head to our favorite summer vacation spot, the Apostle Islands on the shores of Lake Superior. It was there that I outlined the book's contents and pounded out the first draft.

In addition to those I've mentored, I have also been inspired by many great leaders and authors over the years. Classic books from authors Peter Drucker, Michael Porter, and Jim Collins have been invaluable in guiding my journey as a leader. Most recently, authors Peter High and Martha Heller have both written excellent books on IT leadership, and both have been gracious enough to give me feedback about the concepts outlined in this book.

My biggest inspiration for the role of IT Business Partner came from my experience building commercial software for financial institutions. It was then that I learned about product management, user-experience design, and project management. All three disciplines are core to what has shaped my success and the success of many IT Business Partners I have worked with and coached over the years.

I have had the help of many supporters and colleagues along the way, and this book wouldn't have happened without so many giving their time and energy. To all of you, I am forever grateful.

Foreword

I know how important it can be for a new CIO coming from a technical background to get an easy-to-understand, step-by-step roadmap on how to create a successful business partnership for the IT and business organizations. As technology-enabled systems now touch every aspect of a company's mission, CIOs are increasingly expected to be major contributors to company strategy.

What I particularly like about Joe Topinka's approach is it fits perfectly into the project team strategy that companies are finding to be the most productive way to work cross-functionally and with outside-the-company business partners. We live in a virtual world where everything that used to be organized inside the company, within functional departments with clear boundaries of responsibility, is being reinvented around flexible workflow and project team models. Joe Topinka uses his mentoring experience to help CIOs incorporate this thesis into their work plans to drive bottom-line results.

John Sculley, Former Apple CEO

Introduction

IT as an industry is still young. During a keynote address I gave at a recent CIO Executive Summit, I asked attendees for a show of hands if any of their parents had made careers in IT. Only two people out of a couple hundred raised their hands. In some ways, the evolution of the IT industry is in its adolescent phase. IT can sometimes do great things and garner the praise of their company, and then turn around and drive an ERP implementation into the neighbor's tree like an unsteady teenager. IT has still not matured into a full-fledged adult in the opinion of the rest of the company.

In some respects, it could be argued that the role of IT Business Partner is the logical next step in the evolution of IT as a business discipline. In this context, it is understandable that the IT ecosystem hasn't acknowledged the IT Business Partner role in the same way that it has for project managers and business analysts. Universities teach project management, and the Project Management Institute (PMI) offers a certification program, yet there are few, if any, programs that have emerged for the role of IT Business Partner. Similarly, the International Institute of Business Analysts (IIBA) has followed in the footsteps of the PMI. Their goal is to establish a set of standards that could be universally adapted by companies to provide business analysts with a path and a community that supports their career aspirations.

Still, IT leaders themselves have contributed to this dilemma. The very language we use is one obvious but overlooked aspect of why IT attitudes are less than glowing. IT leaders too often refer to internal departments as their customers. In doing so, IT inadvertently sets itself apart from and outside of other functions within the company. It is difficult for business unit leaders to think of IT as a partner when IT positions itself as an internal service provider. It may be subtle, but the old adage "The customer is always right" creates an almost insurmountable barrier to overcome when negotiating with business units. Language like "IT and the business" or "We need a seat at the table" also weakens the perception of IT within companies.

IT leaders so desperately want to be recognized for the strategic value they bring to organizations, and business leaders need to realize the incremental profits that come from business technology convergence. I have spoken to many CIOs and IT leaders about this dilemma, and the idea of a formal IT Business Partnership program as the method to achieve these goals resonates with them. Now is the time if IT is ever going to be valued as a true partner in the business.

Despite the increased awareness of this need, so many of the IT leaders and CIOs that I speak with struggle to get effective and impactful partnership programs implemented in their companies. Martha Heller's *The CIO Paradox* is therapy for CIOs. Her sixteen paradoxes had me nodding my head repeatedly, and it occurred to me after reading the book that IT Business Partnerships represent a kind of CIO paradox, too. CIOs and business leaders talk about "forging partnerships with the business" and yet don't define the role of the IT Business Partner consistently in their organizations. In fact, as industry leaders, we have collectively failed to establish standards for the IT Business Partner role. There isn't a standard job description, industry training program, or certification program available to career-minded individuals. It is no wonder that CIOs haven't defined the role well enough to establish it as a natural part of their company's IT career framework. The role simply hasn't been legitimized in many companies.

While the role is not uniformly defined or implemented in most companies, there is no shortage of discussion around the topic of IT forming close partnerships with the business. Peter High devotes a key principle to the importance of partnering in his book *World Class IT*. In Martha Heller's *The CIO Paradox,* she says CIOs "must tighten your connection to the business." The *Wall Street Journal* recently organized their first CIO Network Conference with global CIOs. When they asked CIOs about their top priorities in the years ahead, number one on the list was "Hardwire IT to the Business" (Bussey, 2013). In IT Business Partnerships: A Field Guide, I provide you with practical, tested methods for truly partnering with the business.

In writing this book, my aim is to help IT leaders implement successful IT Business Partnership programs. I also want to provide readers and inspired leaders with pragmatic and useful tools for immediate use. The goal is for you to use the ideas presented in this book as a starting point for your program, tailoring the processes and methods to your company's culture and style.

Based on my experience, you will need patience. It takes time for programs of this nature to take root. Start with one business unit and try to secure early wins and gain increasing support. Promote your successes and you will likely see more funding and demand for additional IT Business Partners. Flexibility and adaptability will be important attributes to leverage along your IT Business Partner path. I look forward to hearing feedback and stories about your journey.

.

Chapter One

Why IT Business Partnerships Matter

F orrester Research, a global business research and advisory firm, estimates that less than one-third of businesses involve IT in their strategic planning efforts. The consequences of this disconnect almost guarantee that IT organizations merely play a supportive and reactive role in the business process. Put another way, more than two-thirds of companies don't view IT as a strategic partner and don't consider IT in their strategic planning efforts. Forrester often asserts that IT speaks a different language and focuses on metrics and objectives that don't correlate with the rest of the business.

CIO Magazine has been conducting a "State of the CIO" survey for more than a decade. Their most recent survey underscores the poor perception business stakeholders have of IT organizations. Just 15 percent of IT organizations consider themselves business peers, and only 30 percent consider themselves true

The Perception of IT Organizations by Business Stakeholders	Total
Cost Center – *Enterprise value unappreciated, misunderstood or unfulfilled*	21%
Service Provider – *Credible reputation for efficient & effective delivery*	27%
IT Partner – *Trusted, influential collaborator on all things IT*	30%
Business Peer – *Truly part of "the business," engaged in developing, not just enabling, business strategy*	15%
Business Game Changer – *Acknowledged as a primary driver of the enterprise's competitive future*	7%

CIO Magazine's State of the CIO Survey 2012

partners within companies. With such meager strategic influence, IT organizations stand little chance of significantly impacting company performance.

CIOs can change these viewpoints by leveraging IT Business Partners and their knowledge of the business. Seasoned IT Business Partners make the difference between business leaders seeing IT as a connected and strategic arm of the company versus an operational group whose only focus is keeping the lights on. In my experience, the best way to achieve this objective is by demonstrating marketplace knowledge. IT Business Partners that spend time in the field will be readily able to contribute effectively to the strategic discourse.

The elusive role of IT Business Partners has taken on a life of its own in companies globally. Unfortunately, the role isn't consistently defined from one organization to another. In fact, all too often the role isn't formally recognized in HR departments, making compensation and benefits packages hard to benchmark. IT leaders have the desire to partner with their business counterparts, but the IT industry hasn't taken time to establish the role in the same way it has for project managers and business analysts. We even call people serving in the role by different names: IT Business Partner, business relationship manager, IT liaison, client executive manager, even senior business analyst. When inconsistencies like these are the norm, it is no wonder that the role hasn't become an institution in organizations.

The IT industry has reached a point in its maturation where this has to change. There are bottom-line opportunities at stake that IT Business Partners are poised to drive. The sooner the industry recognizes this, the sooner these bottom-line benefits will be realized.

Given the lack of a standard definition for the role of IT Business Partner, let's begin by creating one to provide context for the remainder of the book.

> **IT Business Partner:** An IT Business Partner serves as the chief liaison between IT and associated business units (sales, finance, supply chain, HR, etc.) and as a trusted advisor in developing integrated business and technology investment roadmaps that achieve business unit goals and objectives. IT Business Partners have a strong belief in providing honest, reliable, and market-relevant services to business units.

The Key Functions of an IT Business Partner

IT Business Partners perform a wide range of functions, straddling the fence between IT and business units. In this sense they are bilingual, speaking the language of business and IT. It is essential that they understand where the business is heading strategically, and that they know how to drive business technology investments that help realize the goals of the company.

The following eight functions are central to the role of IT Business Partners:

1. Understand business goals and objectives
IT Business Partners must have a clear understanding of the market and of the financial goals of their company. This fundamental knowledge enables IT Business Partners to determine how IT can help companies strategically.

2. Participate proactively in strategic planning
Proactive involvement during the planning process with business unit leaders deepens the IT Business Partner's understanding of

business goals and creates the most conducive environment for creating solutions that deliver the best possible outcomes.

3. *Meet regularly with external customers*

Unfiltered access to customers offers unique insight into their issues and needs.

4. *Understand the competitive landscape*

IT Business Partners must be armed with a solid understanding of the competition's solutions and value proposition in order to most effectively develop powerful investment roadmaps.

5. *Take an outside-in research approach with customers*

It is imperative that IT Business Partners see their company's products and services in action. There is no better way to see what is working (or not working) than firsthand, in the field. Take an outside-in approach and explore customer touch points from their perspective.

6. *Manage the project intake and governance processes*

IT Business Partners that understand business unit goals, customer needs, and the current state of solutions are best positioned to see which solutions make sense to pursue. IT Business Partner input on cross-organizational investments is essential given the limits on investment funds, ensuring that the best ideas are undertaken.

7. *Develop investment roadmaps*

A natural output of the intake process is an investment roadmap. IT Business Partners must be skilled in identifying the priority of investments that appear on the investment roadmap.

8. *Construct Business Cases*

IT Business Partners must be able to develop the financial aspects of investments, written Business Cases, and related management presentations, all of which are detailed in later chapters.

FUNCTIONAL ROLE SUMMARY

There are many dimensions to the role of IT Business Partner. As staff and executives begin to hear about the role, you will find it useful to have a summary of the eight key functions at the ready. Use the following framework as your guide.

IT Business Partner Functions

Overcoming Unhealthy IT Perceptions

I am sure you hear it all the time: "IT must partner with the business." The assertion is that by doing so, the IT department would be more effective. So why is this so hard to do, and why haven't more IT organizations implemented Business Partnership programs?

Of course, the answer is that it is harder than you think. Not only is IT not considered a part of the business in the same way that sales, finance, supply chain, HR, and other organizational functions are, many executive management teams look at IT as a necessary evil, an organization that sucks cash out of companies with little or no apparent return on investment.

I worked with one executive who liked to say, "I just don't understand IT." Expanding on this sentiment, he would say, "I get what a good finance team looks like or a good sales organization, but when it comes to IT, I am just lost and have to rely on you [I was the CIO at the time] to ensure that we have good IT."

These executives often come from sales or marketing organizations and are quite comfortable when the HR and finance functions report to them. However, it is unusual to find executives who have had IT report to them. As a result, they are tentative about technology and can be intimidated by the complexities and terminology they hear from their IT department.

Frankly, it wasn't all bad that my boss was unsettled by IT; to his credit, at least he was willing to trust me. In his role, he was like many other executives: he had little understanding of IT and what a strong IT Business Partnership program could do for his company.

Getting the Program Right Drives Bottom-Line Results

Implementing IT Business Partnership programs is challenging to say the least, but it is also rewarding. Successful programs drive bottom-line results for organizations that manage to get it right. A 2007 study conducted by the Business Technology Management Institute showed that when companies move beyond basic alignment-level maturity and closer to converged maturity, they enjoy superior economic performance versus their non-converged peers.

Converged Versus Non-converged Peers

Metrics	%
Return of Equity	4%
Return on Assets	8%
Return on Investments	13%
EBITD	7%
Earning per Share	28%
Revenue Growth	11%

BTM Institute Research

Converged maturity means that strategic plans proactively include IT capabilities: IT is part of the strategic dialogue from the outset, rather than the afterthought it usually is at most companies. Based on the numbers above, every financial metric is better for converged versus non-converged companies.

Almost all IT leaders, and business leaders in general, talk about the importance of "aligning IT with the business." This premise is misguided, though, and sets up a dynamic that assumes IT somehow sits outside the business and that special effort is required to bring IT into the fold. What team in any kind of company can afford to operate on this premise? I can't think of one.

The Pitfalls of Alignment

As opposed to determining how to "align IT with the business," the real question should be: How do companies align strategically to build integrated plans, and how do you get all the organizational units rowing in the same direction? The notion that sales and product teams go off on their own, develop strategies, and then plug IT in at the end is the alignment pitfall. This approach is ineffective and lacks the savvy needed to compete in today's global marketplace. IT and other departments (e.g., sales, finance, supply chain, HR, etc.) all need to be involved in strategic conversations from the beginning.

IT is a business unit and a vital part of almost everything companies do. Why, then, does the conversation around IT alignment continue? The answer is simple: leaders let it happen. If you are a CIO, or an aspiring CIO, it is your responsibility to connect the dots between what product and sales teams want to do strategically and the role IT plays in making it happen. If you want IT to be taken seriously as another business unit, rather than cast aside as an outsider, this is your challenge.

The unfortunate fact is that many companies only converse esoterically about needing to align IT and the business. Given that IT leaders touch every business area, they are best positioned to change this tired and ineffective dialogue and turn it into a conversation about the strategic interdependence of teams. I've had success in doing this in the various companies I've worked for over the years. It starts with getting the IT organization connected to customers, sales teams, operations, and call centers. The more IT knows about how the business works, the more clearly they are able to see the challenges facing your company; thus, the better positioned they are to approach these challenges effectively.

Getting plugged in also means IT can have pragmatic conversations with your executive teams about the very real problems and opportunities facing your company, as well as the specific strategies that IT can use to address them. There is no match for firsthand, market-based knowledge, especially when you marry that knowledge with IT solutions that benefit the business.

The Roots of the IT Business Partner Program

I have found the product management principles of the Product Development Management Association (*PDMA.org*) effective as a core foundation for training. These principles orient IT Business Partner thinking toward customers and markets by providing them with a common language that can be shared with product and sales organizations. More importantly, they shift the dialogue strategically. Conversations begin to focus more on the investment portfolio and strategic roadmaps. Additionally, annual budgets and long-range plans become more business-relevant while simultaneously, the IT function is increasingly considered an important and strategic part of the business.

Once established, maintaining a proactive relationship with business units can be an ongoing challenge. This is especially true as new business leaders join the organization. More than likely they will be coming from companies where the IT Business Partner role was not well defined or established. Their perspective on IT could be dated. Their former IT organizations might have been outsourced, or they might not have worked with proactively engaged IT organizations. As a leader, you need to stay on top of these issues to be successful.

Handoffs Are Not Enough

I once had the opportunity to provide an overview of our IT Business Partnership program to a new business unit executive. As it happened, the Olympics had just concluded. She used an analogy from track-and-field to check her understanding of what we were trying to accomplish with our program. She cited the US women's 4x100 relay team that had just set a world record as a metaphor for the type of partnership I was referring to. While there certainly are lessons to be taken from the relay team's achievements, the notion of handoffs between groups just isn't good enough in today's complex business world because it focuses too much on compartmentalized individual performances linked by discreet handoffs. I explained to the executive that we were looking for a much more integrated and interconnected approach that didn't rely on one group relinquishing control to the next.

Having fun with metaphors, I suggested that IT Business Partners work in much the same way bike racers do in a peloton: an integrated team, with everyone playing a role in the process, constantly fine-tuning the shape of their formation to meet the real-time conditions they face, thus creating a graceful, dynamic collaboration.

Let's move beyond metaphors to a real situation: brick-and-mortar retailers dealing with the challenges of transitioning to digital sales, i.e., multichannel commerce. I have seen and heard from many retailers facing the prospect of channel conflict. This is the delicate business situation faced by companies who sell products directly from their e-commerce sites. When this happens, distributors and retailers fear their supplier is suddenly competing for their customers directly. Channel conflict is a very real problem. Companies that have IT Business Partners are better equipped to proactively develop solutions that address both distributor issues and internal process challenges before going live on multichannel commerce platforms.

Imagine a new executive with good intentions is brought in to confront this dilemma. They could spend all the time in the world working with retail operations, sales teams, and dealers to develop a solution without it ever occurring to them to involve IT Business Partners. This is especially likely if they came from an organization devoid of IT Business Partnerships or perhaps one that outsourced their IT function altogether. In this scenario, the new executive's instincts would be to develop a conceptual solution and then hand it off to IT to "make it happen." This occurs over and over in companies today. When it does, IT Business Partners are put in the frustrating situation of playing catch-up with business units.

I am familiar with a retailer where this scenario played out in real time. Their IT Business Partners were handed a solution requiring cumbersome business processes and a new software solution to enable their multichannel program. Their initial program concept was more expensive than it needed to be, it fell short of addressing key customer needs, and it mandated an IT solution based on inefficient business processes.

Had the IT Business Partners been involved up front, the channel conflict approach would have been more easily recognized by all. The solutions would have better addressed key business scenarios for their distributors. They would have avoided the effort required to rework the plan and remap processes, and they could have avoided having to go back and reset distributor expectations.

Imagine this story playing out as it does in most companies. The lost time and missed opportunities add up, negatively impacting the company's bottom-line performance. This is all too common in IT organizations that are merely aligned, rather than converged. Relying on cut-and-dried handoffs between IT and business units is not efficient because it forces IT to chase the business and react to surprises.

The Power of Business and Technology Convergence

In some respects, the relay team concept is similar to aligned IT organizations, and the peloton is illustrative of converged organizations. The business value delivered from the more integrated converged approach goes right to the bottom line according to my own experience and the BTM Institute research, which found that converged organizations outperform their competitors. Completed in 2009, the study revealed that converged business technology organizations sustained a 50 percent bottom-line advantage over non-converged peers.

It is easy to understand why. When strategies are integrated, the right projects are selected by governance teams, and these are more likely to drive solutions to key business challenges. Further, time isn't wasted on projects that don't deliver the right results. Converged organizations also have fewer "last loudest voice" project candidates to filter through, which means that governance teams can be laser-focused on projects that truly matter.

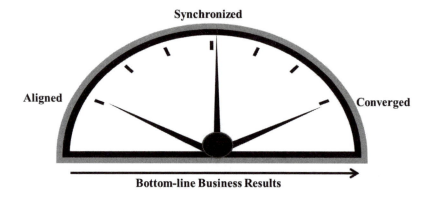

Bottom-line Business Results

As the graphic above shows, bottom-line performance improves when the needle moves from "aligned" to "converged" IT. Many IT organizations strive for alignment, meaning strategic plans are developed and then handed to IT after the fact. This isn't a bad approach; it just doesn't produce the best possible business results. Aligned teams are often in sync with the business. Still, teams that are merely aligned find themselves in the position of playing catch-up with the business too often. More evolved "synchronized" IT organizations typically play a more active role in shaping and influencing how businesses operate, and they drive better results than aligned organizations. However, converged IT organizations are even more sophisticated and have the most impact on bottom-line performance. True convergence happens when business units and IT understand all aspects of each other's needs relative to strategic imperatives. The most successfully converged organizations have effective IT Business Partnership programs, which play a central and critical role in achieving this goal.

When companies move from alignment to convergence, the IT organization's status moves from being an order taker to a true partner, as shown below. Correspondingly, IT's influence and impact are greater as it moves up the power curve.

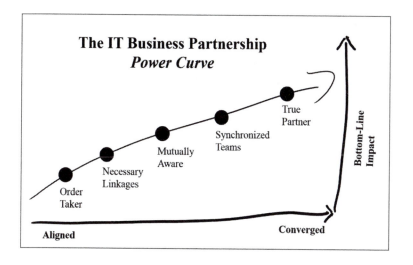

Summary: The Road Ahead

There are many obstacles when implementing an IT Business Partnership program. But when done well, the program will be celebrated by the entire organization. To say this is rewarding is an understatement. These programs help executives see the strategic value of the partnership, and lead to the whole IT organization feeling more engaged. Team members will feel like there is a cross-organizational common cause. With teams pursuing the same goals, IT getting the recognition it deserves, and the entire company enjoying better bottom-line results, it really is easier to get up in the morning and go to work.

Once you commit to implementing an IT Business Partnership program, you will need patience. The journey takes time, and you will need the support of your management team. The marketplace will always present new challenges for IT organizations and IT Business Partners. That is the nature of our free-enterprise system. Nothing lasts forever, and the pace of change has accelerated to unprecedented levels. Getting your IT Business Partnership program up and running

13

will help your company react quickly to rapidly changing market conditions. Choosing the right candidates to spearhead this program is crucial to its ultimate success. The critical skills needed to make your IT Business Partnership program successful are discussed in detail in the next chapter.

Chapter Two

Legitimizing the Role of IT Business Partner

As we review the skills needed to be a great IT Business Partner, you might think I am describing some kind of superhero. IT Business Partners need to understand how the company makes its money, who its customers are, and what motivates these customers to use or buy your goods or services. They also need to understand what can be achieved technologically, and they need to be able to sell their ideas and vision both inside and outside the company.

That certainly seems like a tall order for any one person and frankly, it is. Some of the best IT Business Partners I have worked with have a blend (some better, some worse) of the skills described below. No one person can be a master at them all; however, a good IT Business Partner will seek help in areas where they need it.

IT Business Partner Strengths

If you have read Tom Rath's book *StrengthsFinder 2.0*, the following attributes will seem familiar to you. If they aren't, I encourage you to pick up a copy and take the online self-assessment with the access code included at the back of the book. Rath introduces 34 strengths from which I selected eight. The outline below explains how these eight strengths apply to the IT Business Partner role.

→ **Strategic:** IT Business Partners must possess the ability to see patterns and trends in the marketplace and then develop various scenarios detailing how their company might respond to each of them.

→ *Analytical:* When faced with long and wide-ranging sets of challenges, IT Business Partners have to understand the root causes of these challenges and prioritize which to tackle as part of an investment roadmap.

→ *Connectedness:* A key skill for IT Business Partners is the ability to see connections between events or circumstances that others typically overlook. This ability will prove invaluable in developing a more complete vision and investment roadmap to better enable the company to respond to market needs.

→ *Futuristic:* Getting inspired by possibilities helps IT Business Partners paint a picture of what life could be like with more effective IT solutions. Good futuristic qualities in an IT Business Partner include the ability to be forward-thinking and imaginative.

→ *Relator:* By definition, IT Business Partners work not only with the IT organization but with the other business units they serve. IT Business Partners that relish collaborating with others derive satisfaction and success from selling ideas around the firm.

→ *Communication:* There is no doubt that IT Business Partners have to be great communicators. They will often find themselves presenting to upper management, team members, and customers. Some IT Business Partners take it to another level and blog about what is happening in their company's world. I know some business partners (and CIOs, for that matter) who have been accused of being in sales. When that happens, I generally say, "Thank you!"

→ *Input:* Having a thirst for knowledge drives IT Business Partners out into the field to spend time with sales reps and customers. Because the marketplace keeps evolving, this driving curiosity means it isn't a chore to keep pace with these changes. In fact, it is quite the opposite: collecting ideas and information is rewarding when one can connect the dots and develop an impactful investment roadmap.

→ *Ideation:* IT Business Partners enjoy drawing connections between disparate ideas to form cohesive plans. To sell ideas within the organization, IT Business Partners must know how to effectively link events in the marketplace with the initiatives they recommend implementing.

Of course, there are more skills that IT Business Partners could and should possess. Being able to put things in a historical context, having empathy, being self-assured, and being deliberate are all desirable skills, too. The real key lies in how well IT Business Partners understand their strengths and how they put them to use in the organization. Having a positive, "can-do" attitude helps overcome any shortcomings they may have. The following is a visual summary of the strengths detailed above.

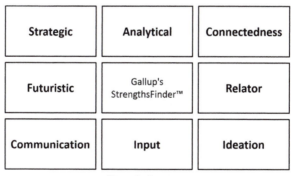

Strategic	Analytical	Connectedness
Futuristic	Gallup's StrengthsFinder™	Relator
Communication	Input	Ideation

Strengths Summary

IT Business Partner Job Description

Building a job description for the IT Business Partnership program will be challenging. There simply isn't an abundance of job descriptions readily available in the marketplace. To complicate matters, the role is poorly understood in most organizations, and little is written about the IT Business Partner function in relevant IT journals or by

IT research analysts. Analysts speak only about the need for IT to get aligned with the business but with no explanation or practical guidance on how to achieve true convergence. Early on, the challenges I faced when trying to implement this role were frustrating to the point that I considered giving it up entirely. Fortunately, I took my own advice, stayed patient, and pressed on.

Because information is not available on this critical role, you will have to tailor the IT Business Partner job description to your company's culture. Your organization may have roles that overlap with the IT Business Partner role described here. That is okay, but you will have to work to identify the overlaps. Working with your HR department and the affected teams to iron out role-based accountabilities will be necessary. You will need someone in IT who is accountable for the business unit/IT relationship, and you will need to get integrated with the company's strategic planning process so that IT can be effectively leveraged. There is no substitute for this. Be prepared to face these types of organizational challenges from the start.

SAMPLE JOB DESCRIPTION

Job Title: *IT Business Partner*
Department: *Information Technology*
Reports to: *Chief Information Officer*

General Purpose of the Job: The IT Business Partner (ITBP) has the overall responsibility of serving as the strategic interface between assigned business units or functional areas for the purpose of business technology strategy development, solution discovery, service management, risk management, and relationship management. The ITBP serves as the business relationship link between business units and IT at the executive level. The ITBP provides highly valued, strategic, consulting-level support and guidance through key IT initiatives. They communicate decisions, priorities, and relevant project information to appropriate levels of staff regarding business unit requests, projects, and initiatives. They proactively share knowledge of technology risks and present opportunities to build competitive advantage by improving the efficiency and effectiveness of business units. They partner with business leadership and other key stakeholders to define opportunities and to prioritize projects based on predefined criteria (e.g., return on investment, productivity, compliance).

The ITBP proactively serves as a "trusted advisor," and is the primary IT point of contact to business line executives and managers. They operate as the key business contact representing IT in promoting IT services and capabilities. The ITBP provides support in delivering technology products that meet the needs of the business. The ITBP also focuses on strategic initiatives and planning activities for their business area. They strive to understand market challenges, including customer priorities and issues related to the competition. ITBPs are proactive and anticipatory in their thinking. They are, by nature, driven and provide significant value to business units. ITBPs facilitate the investment intake process and the high-level planning and execution of business initiatives through the use of technology. They serve a lead role in enabling the business to achieve its objectives through the effective use of technology.

ESSENTIAL DUTIES AND RESPONSIBILITIES:

- → Develop and implement solution roadmaps to ensure successful introductions across the organization and with customers
- → Collaborate with management to develop annual budgets for respective business areas
- → Develop solution concepts and Business Cases for new investments
- → Perform business analysis and prepare recommendations and business plans as needed

→ Create and analyze relevant information and develop recommendations for presenting to senior management

→ Act as the key liaison across all functional areas, including business units, the information technology department, and outside vendors

→ Possess broad knowledge of most technical and business resources and use them to effectively coordinate team members and external resources

→ Create shared vision of their respective solutions and facilitate decision making and arbitration relating to trade-offs both within and between different solution platforms

→ Develop and implement sound rationale for portfolio management and for managing product phase-in/phase-out plans, proactively anticipating gaps and overlaps within the portfolio

→ Create consensus with other functions as to the timing of solution introductions and withdrawals

→ Oversee the launch of solutions and maximize the positive impact on the organization

→ Identify, screen, and evaluate new solution opportunities to address unmet internal and external customer needs

→ Partner with key staff members to create strategic business plans

→ Possess strong analytical skills, including an understanding of business economics and financial resources

→ Utilize the appropriate technologies and ensure that customers have the solutions they need, when they need them, and in the manner best suited to their requirements

→ Collaborate with architecture and operations teams to ensure solution compatibility with company standards

→ Collaborate with the Project Management Office on the intake process and on the prioritization of candidate projects across the company

OTHER DUTIES AND RESPONSIBILITIES:

→ Participate in strategic and budgetary planning processes; prepare and administer unit operating budgets; provide recommendations on desired policies and goals; and implement new/revised programs according to established guidelines

→ Participate in field research in pursuit of new solutions and to evaluate the applicability and effectiveness of current solutions

Customers: Internal and external, business units (e.g., wholesale teams, retail teams, supply chain teams, HR, finance), and key vendors

Education and Experience: Bachelor's degree (B.A. or B.S.) from a four-year college or university or 10 to 15 years of IT and business/industry work experience, with at least three years of leadership experience and five years developing and executing strategic plans and/or project portfolios, or an equivalent combination of education and experience. Bachelor's or master's degree in computer science, business administration, or other related field or equivalent work experience. The Product Development Management Association's New Product Development Professional (NPDP) certification is desirable.

Breadth: Typically has 10 to 15 years of IT and business work experience with a broad range of exposure to various technical environments and business segments. At least three years of experience managing teams responsible for strategic planning, business development, or client management, and at least three years of experience working with a broad range of diverse and complicated business units. The candidate must possess strong business acumen.

The ITBP works with senior-level management, business units, and corporate staff executives to develop a technology strategy that is integrated with IT and across all business units. ITBPs must have a strong understanding of each business unit to include their business drivers for success, processes, and approaches to business models.

ADDITIONAL DESIRABLE QUALIFICATIONS:

→ Strategic thinking and planning
→ Operational execution excellence
→ Nimble LEAN[1] thinking to drive change that enables efficiencies and drives growth
→ Systems thinking
→ Team and collaboration orientation
→ Problem solving
→ Performance driven
→ Learning orientation
→ Public speaking
→ Effective written/verbal communication skills

REQUIRED KNOWLEDGE:

→ Strong written and oral communication skills
→ Strong organizational skills
→ Ability to plan strategically
→ Knowledge of and experience with the Product Development Management Association and/or the Project Management Institute

PHYSICAL DEMANDS:

N/A

WORKING ENVIRONMENT:

→ Some overtime or adjusted hours required
→ Moderate travel required

---

1   LEAN: The Lean Enterprise Institute, Inc. was founded by James P. Womack in 1997.

Instituting the IT Business Partner Role

Establishing the IT Business Partner role as a legitimate function recognized by HR, business unit leaders, and the IT organization is critical to the program's success. Use the following skills matrix and career family placement, in concert with the HR team, to formally establish the role in your company. Consider aligning IT Business Partners directly to the CIO. This gives the IT Business Partner role instant credibility and visibility across the organization. Avoid burying it inside the Project Management Office or in other IT functions.

A common question that IT leaders and business unit leaders ask is, "Can the IT Business Partner be part of the business unit and not part of IT?" My answer is almost always a resounding no. When IT Business Partners are not inside IT, departmental handoffs between business units and IT become the chief method of interacting, making it hard for the Business Partner to achieve business and technology convergence.

Take a look at the summary on the following page to see the skills matrix I use to implement IT Business Partnerships. Keep in mind that you might not have four levels of business partners; I, myself, haven't yet had four levels. The point here is just to give IT Business Partners a clear career roadmap and to give you an idea of how to create this job family in your company. As you read through the role matrix, don't get hung up on the notion that IT has to do everything outlined in the job function. Overlap will occur with existing roles in your company. There is more on this topic in chapter four.

Skills Matrix			
Business Partner I	**Business Partner II**	**Business Partner III**	**Business Partner IV**
Education/Experience or Equivalent Combination			
Bachelor's and/or 3 years	Bachelor's and/or 5 years	Bachelor's and/or 7 years NPDP Training	Bachelor's and/or 10 years NPDP Certification
Technical Knowledge/Depth of Expertise			
• Good business & market knowledge • Basic understanding of data flows & systems integration & reporting systems/tools • Participates in development of new operational ideas • Emerging Project Management skills	• Good business & technical knowledge • Good operational knowledge • Good understanding of data flows & systems integration & reporting systems/tools • Participates in development of new operational ideas • Emerging business case development and financial modeling skills	• Solid business & technical knowledge • Solid operational knowledge • Solid understanding of data flows & systems integration & reporting systems/tools • Drives new operational ideas • Solid business case development and financial modeling skills	• Strong business & technical knowledge • Strong operational knowledge • Strong understanding of data flows, systems integration & reporting systems/tools • Expert at building operational roadmaps • Champions new operational ideas • Excellent business case development and financial modeling skills
Complexity of Problem Solving			
• Collaborates on operational assessments • Basic understanding of system functionality • Contributes ideas for annual business systems enhancement budgets	• Performs operational assessments • Collaborates on operational roadmap development • Solid understanding of system functionality • Collaborates on annual business systems enhancement budgets	• Performs operational assessments • Develops and manages operational roadmaps • Helps facilitate the operational systems intake process • Solid understanding of system functionality • Collaborates on annual business systems enhancement budgets	• Performs operational assessments • Develops and drives operational roadmaps • Excellent understanding of system functionality • Manages the operational systems intake process • Develops annual business systems enhancement budgets
Freedom to Act/Autonomy			
• Normal to limited supervision • Work may be reviewed for accuracy to ensure objectives are met	• Exerts latitude in determining objectives of assignments • Acts independently on defined project tasks • Receives direction from management	• Receives limited direction from senior management • Helps define the operational strategy	• Nearly unlimited latitude allowed and enabled • Independent decision-making ability
Scope of Impact			
• Low to moderate impact	• High impact - Erroneous decisions have immediate impact on operational effectiveness	• High impact - Erroneous decisions have immediate impact on operational effectiveness	• Substantial impact - Erroneous decisions affect operational efficiencies
Internal/External Contacts			
• Works with teams on more detailed aspects of projects	• Works with internal customers • Interacts with operations management • Works with vendors & PMO	• Works with internal customers • Interacts with senior management and business partners • Works with vendors & the PMO	• Collaborates with executive business partners • Maintains relationships with key vendors • Works with the PMO

Job Family

The role of IT Business Partner has a logical place in your overall IT job structure. I use this simple framework to illustrate IT job families and where the IT Business Partner role fits in.

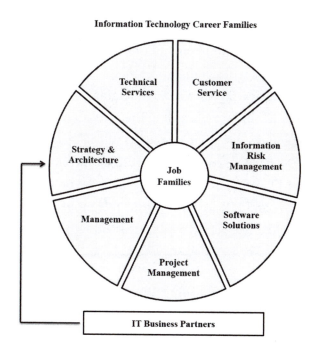

Information Technology Career Families

Summary: Find the Right Candidate and Legitimize the Role

In many respects, choosing the right individual to serve in the role of IT Business Partner will make or break your success. Finding the right person can be a challenge, and you will inevitably get a lot of feedback from peers and business unit colleagues regarding the candidate's qualifications. Before you start looking, or, at a minimum, before you make an offer, be sure to get the position vetted by the executive management team. It is important that they fully understand the strategic nature of the role. The last thing you want is for them to think that IT Business Partners are merely tactical order takers.

Find candidates that have a blend of the right skills. Legitimize the role by making the IT Business Partner a formal part of your IT career family. Collaborate with your HR team to benchmark the compensation and benefits of the role. Work to clarify the role across the company, and be sure to iron out any role conflict issues with other company functions.

The IT Business Partner is an emerging role in IT organizations, and you will face obstacles: The role is not well defined in the industry, and some companies don't value IT and outsource the function. Overlapping company roles cause confusion, and business units shield IT from customers. Stick with the program and work with executive and HR teams to get the role properly implemented so that it will be recognized as a valued and respected function in the company.

How to Legitimize the IT Business Partner Role

1. Get the HR team involved in the process from the start
2. Establish a job description
3. Benchmark the compensation and benefits of the role
4. Identify where the role fits in the IT career family structure

Chapter Three

Structuring the IT Business Partner Function

However you choose to structure an IT Business Partner program, you will benefit by understanding your company's culture and attitude toward structure and process. Pay particular attention to the working styles of the executive and business unit leaders of the company. These styles will help you determine how best to structure your program.

In terms of the reporting relationship, I recommend that IT Business Partners report to the Chief Information Officer. By doing so, you give the role instant credibility and visibility, and send a message to the rest of the company that the role is strategically important and valued. Resist the temptation to have IT Business Partners report to the Project Management Office (PMO). This is something to consider down the road once the program is up and running, but only if your PMO leader has a solid reputation as a forward-thinking business leader both inside and outside of IT.

When launching your program, consider piloting it with a progressive executive or business unit leader. Starting out this way gives you time to experiment and adjust your approach prior to rolling out the program to a broader audience. Be sure the executive sponsor or business unit leader sings the praises of the program to the executive team and the rest of the company.

This chapter explores three structural options for organizing IT Business Partnership programs:

1. Classic Business Unit Alignment
2. Supply Chain Alignment
3. Front-to-Back Office Alignment

The advantages and disadvantages of each option are described below.

Classic Business Unit Alignment

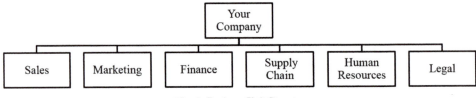

Classic Business Unit Structure

Aligning IT Business Partners to each business unit is a simple but effective approach to structuring the program. This approach creates one-for-one linkages between existing business units and IT, making accountability and responsibility clear from the start. In the beginning there might not be enough staff to cover all of these groups effectively. Consider conducting a trial run with one or two critical groups within the organization. The objective is to demonstrate the effectiveness and impact delivered through the IT Business Partnership process. A good place to start IT Business Partnership programs is in the sales organization. Driving the sales processes and improving customer service brings management visibility to the program.

A potential drawback to the classic structure is that some functions cross business units. For example, companies with multiple brands often have selling organizations that are structured in different business units though they have similar selling needs and Customer Relationship Management tools. IT Business Partners serving these units have to collaborate to balance and prioritize capabilities across these organizations.

Supply Chain Alignment

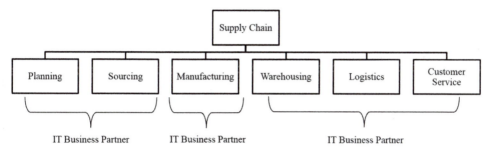

Supply Chain Alignment Structure

In cases where operating units are quite large, it might serve the program well to consider assigning IT Business Partners to separate divisions within a department. For example, supply chain teams are often large and complex. I worked for a consumer goods manufacturer and retailer whose supply chain started with raw materials and finished by delivering products to retail stores and dealers. We assigned IT Business Partners to groupings of departments within the supply chain. All of the Business Partners worked closely together and met frequently to compare notes and brainstorm cross-organizational opportunities and challenges as they surfaced. As the CIO, I made it a point to show my support by taking an active role in the business unit strategy meetings with the IT Business Partners.

Front-to-Back Office Alignment

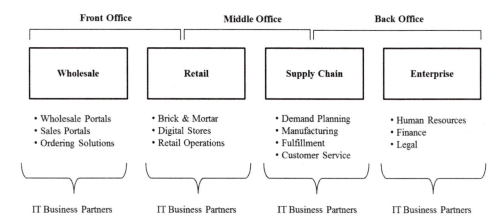

Front to Back Office Alignment

Front-to-back office alignment structures connect IT Business Partners to external and internal audiences directly. The advantage of this structure is that it enables you to organize around user communities. Shaping external user groups is more natural and straightforward and breaks with traditional company organization structures. This option lends itself to thinking more about the holistic customer experience versus a structure that centers on a specific capability or internal department. Field research can be focused on audience needs. For example, field studies that involve dealers will reveal opportunities relating to order management, customer service, promotions, and inventory management.

Roadmaps developed with the front-to-back office structure more naturally connect to the marketplace and make it easier to explain investments to executive management. Consider a set of roadmaps that center on dealers, sales teams, and distributors. Executive management will appreciate a more readily understood focus on user groups. In addition, the investment rationale related to each user group will be less abstract.

One challenge of front-to-back office structures is that there can be capabilities that cross functional boundaries such as order management, inventory management, and payment processing. IT Business Partners must collaborate and take cross-structure capabilities into account when prioritizing investments across the organization. Conflicting priorities will compete for limited dollars. Having a methodology to vet cross-team investments is a key factor of successful IT Business Partnership programs. There is more on this topic in chapter eight.

The Sales and Marketing Challenge

Sales and marketing organizations can also be a challenge when implementing IT Business Partnership programs. This has less to do with their external attributes and more to do with their tendency to consider their viewpoints as representative of the voice of the customer. Over the years, they have grown accustomed to designing websites independently and then handing off requirements to IT for development. In today's marketplace, that model no longer works. The proliferation of social media, cloud computing, and easily accessible information is having a profound impact on customers' expectations of companies, and as a result, on the way companies go to market. The heightened need for integrated and secure customer data mandates proactive collaboration between the IT and marketing teams.

In truth, marketing functions are no different than any other group when it comes to collaboration and its benefits. The marketplace expects companies to operate and perform consistently across all channels. Integrating data from the sales channel to the supply chain, securing that information, and making sure that the customer experience is consistent and relevant across all channels requires a team of astute, market-savvy team members. IT Business Partners must play a key role in charting a course for strategic IT investments that respond to the emerging needs of customers. Marketing departments that opt to run solo will forfeit the opportunity to drive the bottom-line results available via an integrated IT and marketing approach.

Matching IT Business Partner and Business Unit Leadership Styles

As you structure and align IT Business Partners to the organization, think about the work styles and personalities of the leadership team that your partners will be working with. Understanding what motivates the various team members will help you find an IT Business Partner that complements their style. Team dynamics are crucial to a smooth operation. I like to look for candidates that demonstrate strong self-awareness. People who know their own strengths and bring harmony to relationships always seem to do the best job in the role of IT Business Partner. I spend time formally working on team dynamics and team coaching skills. We talk openly about emotional intelligence, individual work styles, and how these attributes can be utilized to enhance business relationships. Leaders tend to be either operationally or strategically focused. Understanding the different approaches of your team members is important when selecting IT Business Partners for these units.

OPERATIONALLY BIASED BUSINESS UNIT LEADERS

I once worked with a supply chain business unit leader who was a hands-down achiever in the Gallup sense of the word. Each day he would detail the tactical challenges facing his team while openly acknowledging his disinterest for strategic planning and roadmaps. He disliked corporate lingo and especially loathed long, drawn-out meetings. He was a doer, not a talker. He self-deprecatingly referred to himself as a knuckle dragger. His pragmatic style and matter-of-fact approach made him fun to work with. Although he was initially indifferent to the new IT Business Partnership program I was implementing, I found two very talented candidates for the function and assigned them to his team. We worked hard to create a roadmap for his organization and won his interest and allegiance for the process when we demonstrated real value by executing the key priorities this leader had for his organization.

We concentrated our efforts behind the scenes, doing our field research and seeing firsthand the problems and challenges facing his organization. We brainstormed ideas to overcome the pain points we uncovered, and we presented them back to his leadership team in a simple, spreadsheet-based roadmap. We organized the roadmap into themes that aligned with his leadership team. As the head of the supply chain, he was charged with continually finding efficiencies to drive margin improvement in the products we produced. We helped him do this through the projects on our roadmap, and we actively participated in his team LEAN events. He soon viewed us as part of his team, which was a major accomplishment. We spoke his language and demonstrated that his priorities were ours, too.

Frequently the projects on our plates were a mixture of mostly operation projects peppered with one or two more strategic initiatives. We put our Project Management Office front and center on the big projects and made sure that the project successes were communicated more broadly to the organization as a whole. We also made sure that the executive team heard about project successes in our monthly IT governance meetings, and we were careful to use only "we" statements when communicating these project successes. At the same time, we purposefully avoided promoting the IT organization too overtly and instead, let our successes speak for themselves. We were sure to take full responsibility for projects that didn't go well. To set an example of what true partners are for the business, we were honest and transparent and willingly shouldered the blame if things went wrong.

The IT Business Partners that I assigned to the supply chain were achiever oriented and appreciated the value of seeing the broader, big-picture roadmap for this team. We used the roadmap as a way to guide the team when priorities shifted, which at times seemed to be a daily occurrence. Our Business Partners did a masterful job of making sure that new projects and requests fit into the roadmap. They worked to minimize project swapping (starting a project and then stopping it for a newer, more urgent one) and explained the cost of this practice without hitting the team over the head with a two-by-four. Nothing turns business units off more quickly than IT espousing the virtues of process and rigor too strenuously. When it comes to process, it is much better to subtly show value and earn trust in the process.

STRATEGICALLY FOCUSED BUSINESS UNIT LEADERS

I once worked with a strategic business unit leader who ran a large sales organization; her leadership style was in stark contrast to that of this now-converted supply chain leader. She loved the business strategy guru Michael Porter and often referred to his teachings during team meetings and strategy sessions. We learned a lot by working with her. To ensure a good fit for her team, I had to find IT Business Partners that could keep up with her strategically but who could also balance getting things done for her organization. This leader didn't like to get bogged down in the day-to-day details, but she did know her numbers. She was always keenly aware of the performance metrics of her group. She knew her sales targets and progress against them, and she knew what her top customer challenges were at all times. Her team pioneered some impactful company-wide programs, one of which involved taking members out of the corporate office and putting them to work in the field, an idea reflected in the CBS television program *Undercover Boss*. Participants got a chance to work in stores, visit customers, and perform the daily duties of a store manager. The program was successful and is still underway today.

I recognized that this leader's strategic approach boded well for the introduction of an IT Business Partnership program, so I launched my new program there first. For her IT Business Partners, I found two relationship-driven individuals. In fact, both asked for training to enhance their strategic skills, and each took the Product Development Management Association's New Product Development Professional training and tested for the formal certification. The skills they learned helped them contribute to the business unit's vision and successes. Representing IT, they actively participated in the business unit's strategic planning process. The business unit leader included them as team members and called them out as such at all company functions.

STAGE GATES

The IT Business Partners described above shared the stage-gate process from the PDMA with the business unit. These stage gates illustrate how we plan in IT and organize our work.

Discover | Initiate | Plan | Execute | Deploy | Close

They liked the process so much that they adapted their own stage-gate process for new business opportunities. They even assigned project managers to key business development initiatives long before these initiatives became projects that involved IT. One business unit leader in particular promoted IT's process innovation and focused her group on initiatives that made the most sense.

SHARED GOALS

To ensure cross-team success, implement shared annual incentive goals in both the IT Business Partner and business unit incentive plans. For example, include business unit revenue or market goals for the year in the IT Business Partner incentive plan and include successful project execution in business unit incentive plans. Think of this as a convergence of goals. This underscores the importance of intertwining IT and business unit incentives, which leads to real business and technology convergence.

Summary: Understand Your Company Culture

Selecting IT Business Partners takes time and patience. Identifying candidates whose style complements the business unit leaders they work with is key to establishing a solid foundation for any IT Business Partnership program. Accelerated program growth occurs when IT Business Partners possessing solid emotional intelligence and relationship-building skills are fully leveraged. It is a good idea to review potential candidates with the head of HR and with senior leaders because they can give an honest assessment of the strengths and potential pitfalls an individual brings to the table.

You might also want to consider starting your program with just one key business unit. Focus on securing early wins and then encourage business unit leaders to laud the value of the partnership to the next business unit. Listen for feedback and meet with your Business Partner team regularly to get their insights into the program. Respond quickly when problems arise. Don't hide issues. Instead, make sure you are transparent with the leadership team about problems as they surface. This will build trust across the leadership team and within the IT Business Partner community. Finally, consider implementing shared incentive goals. Make sure business units and IT Business Partners have reciprocal goals for each other in their annual incentive plans. There isn't a foolproof method for selecting candidates, but these basic guidelines greatly improve your program's chances of success.

Chapter Four

Obstacles to Implementing IT Business Partnerships

There will be many obstacles when implementing an IT Business Partnership program for the first time in your company. For example, everyone you come into contact with brings their work history and biases with them. You will encounter executives that come from organizations that outsourced IT, that implemented roles with overlapping responsibilities with the IT Business Partner function, and who resist the idea of engaging IT staff in face-to-face customer meetings. Likewise, IT can be too rigid and inflexible, leading to business unit frustration and friction. What follows is a summary of four common obstacles that I have faced when starting a new Business Partnership program.

Reliance on Outsourcing

A large, top-tier retailer recently outsourced all of its IT to one of the big accounting consultancies. Outsourcing to that extreme has made it difficult for this retailer to maximize IT's power strategically, and now, four years after their decision, they are still frantically trying to recover from their mistake. Such decisions are driven by the misguided belief that IT is a commodity service and that no differentiation comes from the function. Today, this big-box retailer is fighting for its life.

The mindset of IT as an expense-riddled, cash-sucking commodity is still very much alive, and keeps coming to the fore, especially when the economy dips. You will need to be on the lookout for warning signs of this happening. Your ability to get the IT Business Partner role defined internally in a way that complements already existing roles will be crucial to successfully establishing IT Business Partnership programs in your company. If another group is performing the function well, find a way to proactively collaborate with and participate in that specific function. Beware, though: the unenlightened will try and put IT back in the basement if you are not careful.

Conflicting Roles

In recent years, a number of well-intentioned organizations have defined an emerging product manager role in the e-commerce world. The role goes by many names, including "Digital Product Manager," "E-commerce Product Manager," "Web Product Manager," and even "Capability Manager." These roles clearly have overlap with the classic product management role. Understanding the differences will be important in shaping the role of the IT Business Partner at your company. One big challenge with these emerging roles stems from e-commerce groups essentially carving out an organizational island within companies and focusing on a specific business function, typically e-commerce related. When this happens, it is frequently true that corporate IT organizations are cut out of the conversation, making it difficult to achieve true business and technology convergence. Tier-one retailers are famous for creating self-contained dot. com organizations that focus solely on e-commerce capabilities. Self-contained e-commerce business units have proven they make the already daunting task of implementing a true multichannel retail solution considerably more challenging.

The issue is that business technology has a direct impact on shaping a company's brand. Carving out teams and not integrating them into the overall strategic operation inevitably creates market-based problems down the road. Customers expect their brand experience to be the same regardless of where or how they do business with a company. IT Business Partners working collaboratively with business units ensure that the market solutions shaping customer experiences are consistently delivered across all channels. This can only happen if business and technology teams work together from the very beginning.

When business units push to create separate e-commerce teams, they may be doing so as a result of one business unit manager's dissatisfaction with IT. If they view IT as a hindrance or a roadblock, they will be motivated to find alternatives to getting things done. How many times have you heard business unit staff say, "I don't care about your process, I have a business to run"? To avoid this, IT must be seen as responsive to business units and customers, while simultaneously balancing the need for process and control. IT Business Partners make this happen by acting as business unit advocates.

IT: Its Own Worst Enemy

Early in my IT Business Partnership journey, I took a rigid view of the role IT played in developing business technology strategy and probably had more passion for the process than I did for actual results. This turned out to be a hindrance in getting the role accepted more broadly by the company I worked for. If you are viewed as a purist, people will resist the broader vision of getting IT integrated into the business. This is an example of IT working against itself. IT Business Partners can go a long way toward solving this conflict by creating bridges and emphasizing shared goals between business units and IT.

The Only Voice of the Customer is the Customer's Voice

Business units like to say that they are the voice of the customer. They want to own and control all aspects of customer interaction, including customer requirement handoffs to the IT organization. This is one area where there should be no compromise. No one group can claim to be the voice of the customer, because the only voice of the customer is the customer's voice. Everyone in your organization should jump at the chance to meet and interact with customers. There is no better way to see how things are working than by being in the field and seeing firsthand what customers are experiencing. IT Business Partners have to get out into the field and into the natural habitat of the customers to see what life is like for them as they interact with a company and its technology. The in-depth knowledge and perspective gained from being in the field can't be gleaned by outsourcing or summarized in a memo. Directly observing customers is the "secret sauce" when it comes to designing the right technology solutions for any given business.

Summary: Overcome Your Obstacles

Implementing IT Business Partnership programs is challenging. Keep an open mind and be creative when solving the problems you encounter. Remember, executives bring their work history and IT perception biases with them to every organization. Find a way to harness role overlap when conflicting roles are uncovered. Remain flexible and adaptable when defining processes relating to the IT Business Partnership program. Holding the line on process will only serve to frustrate business unit executives and leave them with the impression that your organization isn't collaborative or nimble. Make it safe for business units to plug IT Business Partners into customer conversations. This is crucial when it comes to establishing trust with the business unit and defining solutions that are right for the market. IT Business Partners can overcome the obstacles outlined in this chapter by being the champion for shared goals between business units and the IT organization.

Chapter Five

Seeing Is Believing:
The Importance of Field Research

How many times have you heard someone say, "I am the voice of the customer"? When I hear this it makes me cringe. In my experience, people who say this are relying on anecdotal data as the basis of their grand statement. While their intentions might be good, such proclamations lead to an "us-versus-them" dynamic between IT and the other business units. As discussed in chapters three and four, the only voice of the customer is, in fact, the customer's voice, and the best way to hear that voice is firsthand. According to *CIO Magazine*'s 2012 State of the CIO Survey, a meager 23 percent of CIOs meet with external customers as a way to improve business relationships with stakeholders. This is an abysmal statistic and a strong indicator of the need for change.

Field research has had a more significant impact on the way I think about solving problems in business than any other technique I have come across. There is a wealth of information to glean from being in the field, seeing things with your own eyes and listening with your own ears. The discipline of field research isn't a new one; it has been a key tool of user-experience professionals for many years. Their powers of observation have been honed to a fine point, and the solutions they produce are simple and elegant. When a website or mobile application is particularly easy to use, people often react by saying, "What's the big deal? That doesn't look so hard!" What these people overlook are the design skills of good user-experience design professionals, who incorporate field research and observation into the development of powerful user experiences.

Hide the Technology, Surface the Work

Early in my career I was fortunate to work with pioneers in the field of user-experience design. My introduction came while working for a major financial services company that provided licensed software and services to banks across the US and around the globe. In my role as a business unit manager, I was responsible for product management, software development, sales, and customer support for the products in my area. I helped build several software solutions that the largest banks in the country still use in their operations today. Prior to learning about user-experience design, I thought I knew how to build great software. My underlying solutions had solid data and software architecture, though the user experience was not the best it could be. That changed when I had the chance to work with a team of user-experience design pioneers that had honed their skills at Apple Computer in the early days of Macintosh. They introduced the concept of user-experience design to our company. We took their teachings to heart, and the company built a usability lab to teach the principles of good user design around the firm.

I will always remember this user-experience team's mantra of "hide the technology, surface the work." That principle makes a lot of sense, but it can only be achieved if there is an understanding of what the "work" is. The best way to gain an understanding of the "work" is through firsthand observation via field research. The user-experience team shared a video with us that is still fresh in my mind, even after all these years. It featured a new Macintosh PC owner enthusiastically opening the box only to discover an intimidating collection of manuals and documents. The video showed the customer leafing through masses of paperwork until they finally found the document labeled "Read Me First." The Apple team had also thoughtfully included a one-page quick start guide, but this document was not one of the first things the happy new customer saw upon opening the box, either. Rather, it was buried in the middle of the stack of manuals and documents.

The video we watched was taken as part of the usability process the company is still famous for. Of course, their findings led to a different packaging solution, and the "Read Me First" and quick start guides were positioned so they would be the first thing customers saw when they opened a new Macintosh.

Apple wasn't the first company to take user-experience design to heart, but they were the first to make it such a visible and commercial success. What is surprising is that it took so long for user-experience design to become a staple in software design and a core business function in companies. Apple was one of the earliest to leverage the power of observation, and IT Business Partners need to master this skill in their roles too.

User-experience design is often relegated to user-experience design teams. I would argue that IT Business Partners should actively participate in the process. User-experience professionals look for key stakeholder involvement in field research. They recognize that bringing different perspectives to the table yields better results. IT Business Partners who make field research a priority give themselves a leg up over those who don't spend time in the field. Researchers know from interviewing people and then seeing them in action that what we say we do rarely matches what we actually do. The implications of this disparity are huge and not to be underestimated in the context of solving business challenges. Frankly, this phenomenon isn't unique; it is similar to the discrepancies between people's self-reported and actual eating habits or sexual activities. A thorough understanding of the disparities between what people say they do and what they actually do even has a bearing on shaping effective public policy. The same is absolutely true when shaping IT solutions.

Lessons from the Field

Observing customers in their natural habitat provides the information needed to build solid investment roadmaps. Make sure to get the IT Business Partners involved in the design team's user-experience processes. Leverage their powers of observation and enlist them to strategize solutions to the problems uncovered in the field. This sets up IT to act from a position of expertise, commanding authority that it couldn't otherwise have achieved. Management and executives in general respond well to this level of powerful, firsthand knowledge. There is no better way to produce these insights than with in-person field research.

Technology requirements are often unspoken. While working for a major accounting firm, we conducted field research to see what we could learn about the problems facing our auditors when they were on location at our customers' offices. We interviewed people ahead of time and had a comprehensive list of the issues we thought we would encounter in the field. When we got on site, however, we uncovered many new issues that hadn't come up during our pre-visit interviews.

We learned that when people encounter technology problems, they develop inefficient workaround processes that are initially frustrating but prove necessary to getting the job done. Over time these workarounds just become so ingrained that users don't even remember the steps clearly when recounting them in an interview. In fact, they often skip steps and don't mention the inefficiencies they are dealing with because these inefficiencies have become routine. It was common for our auditors to gloss over software glitches and inefficient technology solutions, especially when they had been dealing with them for years. Once we knew about these situations we asked the auditors why they'd put up with these headaches. More times than not they told us that they used to report the problems in the early years but that no one listened and so they gave up. Eventually they developed their own workarounds, thereby masking the issues and hiding a deeper frustration with both the technology and with the organization's failure to deal with these problems.

Another lesson stems from my involvement in building a web-based brokerage workstation for a large securities clearance and settlement firm. This product was used by retail broker dealers across the country. Our user-experience team spent a considerable amount of time in our customers' offices. We developed a complete set of working prototypes and took them out in the field to get feedback from brokers. We took the "hide the technology, surface the work" philosophy to heart. Our solution was targeted at investment advisors. Brokers typically worked in an open cubical environment with a lot of commotion. They had to contend with numerous phone calls, frequent market alerts, and a constant stream of people stopping by to chat. We knew our solution had to get them the information they needed in a format that was easily accessible amid so much distraction.

These brokers were commission based, so they liked to check how well they were doing many times every day. Trying to be helpful, we created a portal in our web-based solution where they could see their commissions in real time. This information was prominently displayed on the home page of our solution. Once we got in the field to observe the brokers in action, however, we quickly realized how private they were about their commission results. We saw them frantically clicking on other windows to hide their performance information any time another broker was in the vicinity. It was immediately obvious that we needed to create a simple toggle button on the commission data. If another broker walked by, they could simply click on the button to hide the data; similarly, this button allowed them to quickly expose more pertinent data when serving a customer. This seemingly simple, observation-based improvement created a lot of buzz and was heralded by brokers as the one thing they liked most about the product. This is a prime example of an unspoken requirement. It wasn't something they would have ever thought to articulate on their own. Only through field observation was this critical privacy requirement revealed and met, much to the relief of the brokers.

Field research doesn't always have to be done in association with a specific project or investment initiative. There are many ways to engage with customers in the field. One approach successful companies increasingly take is sending employees out in the field to experience firsthand what it is like to serve customers with their existing technology and business processes. The premise behind these types of programs is simple: give corporate employees a taste of what it is like to actually service customers using real, everyday processes and tools. For example, corporate employees gain unparalleled insight into what it is like to serve customers when they ring up sales tickets, process returns, take inventory, and perform everything store personnel typically do on a daily basis.

I have seen these programs highlight frustrations experienced by new, typically younger, employees as they learn how to use their company's systems. While I was visiting a store during one field research exercise, a manager happened to be training new employees. It quickly became apparent that the user experience for new employees of this store wasn't natural compared to their previous technology experiences. In their personal lives these new staff members were well acquainted with navigating smartphones, laptops, and even touch-screen tablets. But while training to use their company's systems they had to memorize what felt to them like convoluted transaction paths and non-intuitive codes. Not only was this frustrating for them, but new employee training took longer than necessary, so it was more expensive than it had to be. Given the relatively high turnover rate and scarce resources in the retail industry, anything making it more difficult or expensive to attract and keep new employees has immediate business implications. The field research team was delighted to find an opportunity for IT to simplify the user experience and reduce the effort and expense required to train new staff. Based on the field results, they put together a list of requirements that met the needs of typical new employees, and then used these requirements to guide their search for a new system. The field staff welcomed the new system with overwhelming enthusiasm, and the initiative was a success. Without the perspectives we uncovered during that field research, it is unlikely that the research team would have seen the need to replace critical business systems that they had previously thought were working just fine.

Summary: Make Field Research Routine

Corporate employee field research programs should become a permanent fixture at every company. These programs are impactful and well worth the time. From an IT perspective, staff learns what is and isn't working with both software and business processes, and invariably uncover long-standing but under-reported IT system inefficiencies. Visiting staffers have a short window of time to see the challenges firsthand. This means all the technology problems are still fresh in their minds, allowing them to more accurately detail even small glitches in technology tools to a degree that the people who habitually work in the field cannot do.

Employee programs like these do more to give corporate staff members a taste of what it is like to work in the field than any other initiative, and circumvent the human tendencies toward acclimation and erroneous self-reporting. These programs create lasting bonds with field personnel and raise awareness and sensitivity to what it is really like to serve customers. This couldn't be accomplished with a memo from management or a PowerPoint at a company quarterly meeting.

The most salient benefit I have seen emanate from employee field research is a heightened awareness among the corporate staff: they develop an ability to anticipate the financial implications and emotional impact that new policies, processes, and solutions might have on field personnel. IT Business Partners must make field research a priority within their company. Visit internal departments, sit in on the call center, see how the payables department does their job, spend some time in packing and shipping, or in other operational areas. In other words, get out there and see what is happening firsthand.

Chapter Six

Field Research Example: A "Day in the Life"

This chapter details a real-world example of how field research can be leveraged to drive positive change and business results, and examines the use of storytelling with graphics as a method for communicating the challenges employees and customers face when working for or interacting with your company.

I was hired by the president of a top-tier accounting firm a number of years ago who wasn't an accounting professional by trade. He was an excellent strategic thinker, and he brought a growth-oriented mindset to a company that had historically been comfortable growing at an unhurried and predictable pace. He introduced business development and performance measurement programs that began to move the needle on growth.

Historically, the organization had grown through the acquisition of regional US accounting firms. One acquisition, however, quickly changed our direction. We merged with a large accounting firm that nearly doubled our size in revenue, employees, and offices. This catapulted the company to the fore, making it the fifth largest audit and tax firm in the country. They did a masterful job consolidating acquired firms onto a common audit and tax platform, especially considering that our audit software had been in place for close to ten years when I arrived on the scene as their first CIO.

Growth Brings Challenges

Growth brought new obstacles to the company. The acquisitions highlighted cultural challenges, as well as problems with the business process and tools. With so many audit professionals coming from diverse backgrounds and using different audit software solutions, the organization was under considerable pressure to rethink its tools and business processes. In addition, our rapid growth put stress on the professional staff to deliver better results every year. Unfortunately, the combination of cultural issues, outdated tools, and non-standard business processes contributed to high turnover, leaving the leadership team searching for answers.

Like many other firms, this company didn't look at IT strategically. The IT organization was considered a cost to be managed. The partners didn't see the value of making IT an important part of the firm's operation. When I arrived, IT wasn't even included in the firm's annual capital planning process, making initiatives involving IT an afterthought. Our challenge was to figure out how the IT organization could solve the most pressing obstacles facing the firm. In other words, how could we get the leadership team to listen to us, and how could we present them with the problems our auditors were facing in the field? Naturally, we turned to field research. We knew that the problems, and ultimately, the solutions to those problems, were out there waiting for us if we only could uncover them.

We launched a comprehensive field research effort with the simple goal of finding out what was making life difficult for our professional audit staff as they worked in the field with customers. Our IT Business Partners worked with the managing partner of the audit practice to identify the offices we might visit and the engagements that made the most sense to observe. We settled on a combination of twenty cities and audit engagements, traveling from New York to

California and back. We saw audits in action, we watched partners review audit results—we even watched our customers watching our audit teams. The findings were revealing.

Once the field visits were complete, we examined everything that we found. We looked for patterns and themes. Some of the most impactful elements of our research were the quotes we captured when talking to partners, audit professionals, and executives along the way. Our employee and customer comments told a story of frustration and confusion. They also told one of commitment and compassion. Our audit teams were dedicated to their work. Our customers clearly saw that and responded favorably to these committed professionals. They also could see the challenges our audit teams faced. They saw volumes of paper, aging technology, and a proliferation of wires and cords jammed into their conference rooms. They saw auditors struggling with the technology as they worked late into the evening to get their work done. It became clear to us that the tools we armed our teams with were having a negative impact on our company's brand, employee turnover, the attitudes of employees and customers, and ultimately, profits.

Quotes from the Field

Below are examples of the comments we heard, all of which highlight the adage "You can't make this stuff up!" These quotes summarize the problems and frustrations our employees and customers were experiencing every day.

- → Office leader: "People talk as though we are falling behind; we already have."
- → Auditor who had returned after leaving the firm: "It is hard to come back to work here after being at a competitor."
- → Partner: "We've lost deals because we haven't been able to respond to proposals while on the road."

→ Partner: "The most frustrating part of my job is spending three to four hours out of a day messing with technology."

→ Partner: "Dragging a field server around is limiting and cumbersome."

→ Auditor: "We save every three to five minutes to make sure we don't lose data."

→ Auditor: "When we call into the help desk, they just keep telling us to restart."

→ Auditor: "We have to unplug the client's fax machine and take turns connecting to the web over a dial-up connection."

→ Tax partner: "How can we leverage employees with each office doing their own thing?"

Pictures Tell the Story

The pictures we took while on the road underscored what we found during our research. For our purposes, they were truly worth a thousand words.

With all of the field research in front of us we had to figure out a way to tell executive management the story of what we had uncovered. The amount of data we collected was too voluminous to share as captured. We began by looking for recurring themes from our field research. This is what we found:

→ Information was hard to find.

→ There were significant mobility constraints.

→ Employees didn't have a sense of employee community.

→ Tools had fallen behind those of the competition.

→ It cost too much to deliver our services.

With these themes in hand, we began to iterate solutions to address them. We knew we couldn't fix all of them all at once. Instead, we developed a roadmap that addressed the key themes we uncovered. We turned to storytelling as a vehicle to deliver our message, and wrote a "Day in the Life" strategy document formulated around five "what-if" statements:

✓ What if everything an employee needed to perform their job was available to them anytime, anywhere?

✓ What if our tools and processes went from industry-lagging to industry-leading and became a competitive advantage?

✓ What if access to technology and tools were a reason employees chose to come to our firm, and made it harder for them to leave?

✓ What if we had a single view and a single system of record for a customer?

✓ What if the tools, systems, and determination were available now to achieve these goals in a cost-effective manner?

These "what-if" questions opened the door to new possibilities. In effect, they allowed people to think beyond the struggles they faced every day, or in some cases, for many years. It allowed them to imagine a new world free from the frustrations and constraints they had been forced to endure.

Our storytelling approach leveraged real-life situations from our field research. We set these stories in the future (post investment) to give management and employees a new perspective on what life at the firm would be like if investments were funded to solve the problems. Our strategy document also contained a one-page summary corresponding to each "what-if" question.

Here is a sample of what Goal 1 looked like:

Goal 1	**What if everything an employee needed was available anytime, anywhere?**

	Objective 1.1: Access to the company from Client Offices	**Measurements & Expected Outcomes:**
	Strategies:	
"We've lost deals because we can't respond to proposals while on the road." — Partner	• Roll out updated VPN • Create an Intranet available over the Internet to access client tools, phone books, sales and marketing information	• Increase in chargeable hours per employee • VPN uptime and availability measured and improved
"We have to unplug the client's fax machine and take turns connecting to the web over a dial-up connection." — Auditor	• Establish a "Wireless War Room" with laptops and printers all connected via latest technology	• Employee-wide survey results on Technology to improve from 5 worst responses to top 5 responses
	Objective 1.2: Access to email anytime, anywhere	
"I don't know where to find phone numbers and I am not sure what office people are in unless I go to Notes and type the name into an email message." — Marketing	**Strategies:** • Migrate to Web-based Email • Email access via mobile devices	• Reduction in turnover based on access to improved tools

The "Day in the Life" strategy document worked well, but it didn't clinch the deal. We needed to make even more of an impact. One of our most creative team members saw an advertisement in a trade magazine for a company that specialized in taking complex problems and messages and simplifying them into easy-to-digest graphics. We decided to take a chance and asked them to help us communicate our message with the hope of getting our investment funded. We spent a few days showing the firm what we'd uncovered. We shared our "what-if" document and field research, including all the quotes we had amassed. In return, they created a visual placemat that encompassed most of the key messages we wanted to deliver to upper management.

This company taught us that in order to sell an idea you have to get the decision makers to feel the pain of the problem. You have to show them how to overcome the problem and then give them a glimpse of the future. As it turned out, our storytelling and "what-if" documents had many of the elements needed to paint the right picture, and formed the foundation of a cartoon graphic of our story. The graphic was simple and elegant, but it wouldn't have been possible to create the cartoon without the firsthand observations we gleaned during our field research.

I have included a sample graphic to illustrate the power of the picture. On the left side of the cartoon we tell the "Pain of Today" story. These vignettes came directly from the field research. Together with the quotes from the field, the pictures and captions tell the story of outdated technology, long hours, high turnover, and inadequate business technology.

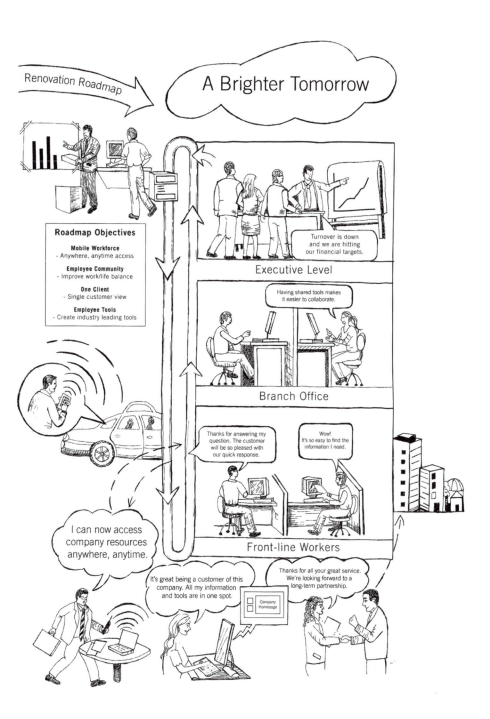

THE ROADMAP TO THE FUTURE

The middle section of the cartoon shows a simple roadmap that leads to a glimmering tomorrow. The roadmap is straightforward and highlights the key investments that, if made, would lead to a better world for both employees and customers. In our case, we proposed new mobile technologies to help people connect while on the road, new tools to perform audits, new tools to enable employees to connect with one another, and a new executive process to ensure a path forward for future investments.

The right side of the cartoon is the bright new world our company would experience after the investments were made. It highlights improvements and solutions to the woes described on the "Pains of Today" side of the picture. The cheeriness of the graphic draws the viewer's attention and is compelling. Who wouldn't want to work in a company that had all the right tools to serve customers in a first-rate way?

With our "Day in the Life" strategy document and cartoon completed, we still had to find a way to convince the management team to take the investment plunge. We set up a large conference room in our offices with artifacts from our field research and the cartoon. We invited our executive team and employees to take a stroll through a "Day in the Life" of an auditor. In the conference room we had three walls to work with. We made the wall on the right side of the room our "Quotes from the Field" display wall. We created poster-size cutouts of key quotes from our field research so that our management team couldn't avoid seeing what staff members had to say about working for our company.

We hung a twenty-foot-wide version of the cartoon on the back wall of the conference room. At first it was a challenge to get the executives to read all the quotes from the field because they immediately wanted to know what the giant cartoon was all about. However, once they started reading the sobering quotes, they momentarily forgot about the cartoon picture draped across the back wall.

On the left wall, we assembled working prototypes of the solutions we were proposing. We had smartphones with speech access to email and voicemail, wireless air-cards that the audit staff could use to connect to the office while on the road, and much more.

Once the executives made their entrance, it didn't take them long to feel the pains of today. The quotes from the field turned out to be incredibly convincing. Some executives read and reread them, asking us if the quotes were actually real. Of course they were, and that was why they were effective in connecting the executives to the frustration and pain our teams felt every day on the job. Once we made it through the quote wall, we took them on a tour of the cartoon. This really put things into perspective. We showed pain points at virtually every level within the organization, and shared our roadmap and vision, giving them a glimpse of what the future could hold.

The prototype demonstrations helped the executives see that the proposed solutions were real and pragmatic. They were fascinated by the possibilities. All we needed to do was convince them that IT could make the solutions happen if they would just give us the funding. They were hooked at this point. The "Pains of Today" cartoon and the field research quotes compelled them to authorize the funding needed so we could begin changing the course we were on as a firm. It was an exciting and rewarding time for everyone working on the project.

Management eventually asked us to take our show on the road. We presented the "Day in the Life" strategy with our big twenty-foot cartoon at the annual partners meeting and took it with us to key offices around the country. The response was positive and overwhelming because we found such a powerful method to articulate and address the problems.

Summary: Seeing Is Believing

I have since used the "what-if" approach and cartoon graphic concept to secure funding for key investments at other firms. People usually cite the cartoon as the definitive component of my presentation, but I always remind them that the field research behind the results is actually the key. Our team could not have come up with the "what-if" strategy document or created the cartoon graphic without it. If I can leave you with only one message after reading this book it is that you must get out in the field. You will not likely discover market developments or buried problems from a focus group or trade magazine. IT Business Partners just have to get out there and observe things with their own eyes and ears. The answers to most questions will be found out there, in the real world, where teams and customers live every day.

A big part of what made the cartoon image work in our company was that it told the truth. It was an unvarnished look at the tools and methods our staff had at their disposal while serving customers. Our managing partners spent a lot of time analyzing quantifiable market data, billable hours, metrics, and more. What they missed in all of that analysis was the truth about what life was like in the field. All the analytics in the world couldn't reveal the emotional reality of what employees were feeling as they serviced our customers. Thanks to field research, we were able to see and hear their pleas for help. Our cartoon image was an emotional mirror for the staff. When they saw it they knew we had heard them loud and clear. There was no whitewashing or minimizing the truth. We powerfully leveraged their stories and experiences in the cartoon and in our strategic plan. And, bottom line, our IT Business Partners earned these employees' trust.

IT organizations and their IT Business Partners that use field research to frame impactful storytelling will have an easier time getting their company to achieve business and technology convergence. Without this research, the IT Business Partnership program is unlikely to keep its seat at the strategy table.

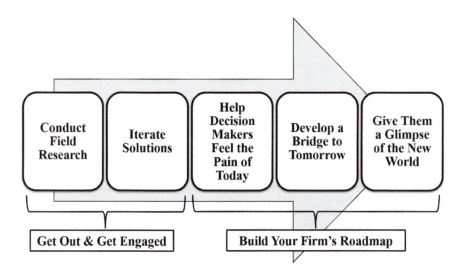

The "Day in the Life" Journey

Chapter Seven

Words Matter: The Power of Language

I f you have worked in IT for any length of time, you have probably heard someone utter a variation on one of the following phrases:

→ "IT and the business should be aligned."
→ "IT and the business should be in sync."
→ "We should connect IT's strategic plans with the business."

As IT continues its maturation process toward being acknowledged as a core business discipline, more people are recognizing that IT is a business unit and not some separate entity to be treated differently. Still, IT organizations are often just as guilty as anyone of perpetuating this "us versus them" mentality by the language they use in everyday meetings and through interactions with other business units. Utterances such as "IT and the business" present unnecessary barriers for the IT Business Partnership program and encourage the uninformed to treat IT less respectfully than they should; such language also makes it harder for business leaders to see the value that strategically integrated IT and business unit organizations bring to the table. Separate but equal actually means separate and unequal. Avoid using language that separates IT from the business.

IT Catch Phrases

Instead of saying "IT and the business," use the name of the department in everyday language, such as "IT and sales" or "IT and marketing." I also encourage staff members to be open about this intentional choice of words with the other business unit leaders in the company. They should know why you are using this specific language and how they can use it to help the company's business overall. The idea is to subtly perpetuate the fact that IT is a business unit and a critical one at that. Using this type of proactive language cements IT's role as a critical component of the company's operation and will lift some of the negative perceptions that non-IT leaders have of the IT organization. IT Business Partners are on the front lines of this dialogue, and they need to be consistently firm in their communication of IT's significant role in the company's operation.

Using the phrase "IT and its customers" is also a bad idea. IT organizations should not refer to their partner business units as "their customers." This automatically puts IT in a weaker position. The old adage "The customer is always right" is alive and well in most people's thinking, and makes it hard for business unit leaders to consider IT an equal partner as opposed to merely a service provider. Being aware of this has helped me make a simple but powerful change in the language choices I make as a leader in IT organizations. The results have been overwhelmingly positive.

You will know you've had success outside of IT when other business unit leaders begin making it a point to get the IT organization involved in strategic conversations early in the process. It is so rewarding when this begins to happen consistently. Momentum will build as the early adopters help other business unit leaders see the light.

Saying Yes to Projects

Managing the request intake process is one of the principal responsibilities of IT Business Partners. IT's reputation is shaped by how end user requests are handled. Let's take the simple word "no." IT Business Partners don't like to say no to requestors, and conversely, people requesting projects don't like to hear "no" when it comes to their project ideas. This chapter explores techniques that will help end users understand their responsibility to the organization when requesting projects, and details the language IT Business Partners can use to manage their expectations.

A chief focus area for most IT organizations is the success rate of the projects they undertake. Choosing the right projects to work on is as central to the company's success as the PMO's ability to execute projects once they are undertaken. The question is how to accomplish this when end users are clamoring for more and expressing frustration at not getting their projects prioritized. No doubt you have had people from around your company asking about a project they submitted many years ago. They ask, "When will my project get done?" or "Why haven't we started it yet?" Typically there is frustration or even disdain in their voice. Even though they might not say it outwardly, you can almost hear them thinking, *Don't you get it? My project is important! I don't care what else is on your plate—that's your problem! Just get my request done!* It seems that the longer the idea marinates in their minds, the better they think their ideas have become.

In these cases, end users erroneously believe they do not have to justify the value of their requests. They feel entitled to a solution just because they asked, or by virtue of the fact that they have been long-suffering for years, waiting for their project to finally be tackled. In reality, IT Business Partners must help end users gain perspective on the business benefits of their requests. Simply put, there are only three broad reasons projects make the grade: they produce more revenue, save money, or mitigate risk. IT Business Partners need to ask requestors how their ideas address these areas. Here are a handful of sample questions to ask:

→ Can you clearly articulate the value of your idea?
→ What has prevented forward movement on your project in the past?
→ What are the roadblocks and what have you done to overcome them?
→ Have you had a partner in IT to help get your idea through the vetting process?
→ If so, where did the process break down?

HELP END USERS SEE PROJECT DRIVERS

IT Business Partners can help end users see that they are closest to a project's business drivers. With an IT Business Partner at their side, end users will be re-empowered to get their ideas into the project intake process successfully. IT Business Partners can also help users see that their projects will be evaluated on both their own merits and within the larger context of all other possible projects. IT Business Partners need to be seen as supportive watchdogs, listening for good project ideas and helping end users get their ideas moving when the ideas are worth evaluating further.

COMBATING THE "DEPARTMENT OF NO" REPUTATION

IT oftentimes earns a reputation of being the "Department of No." Companies have finite resources, and not every project can reasonably be undertaken. It is easy to see how IT gets labeled with this negative and undeserved reputation, even when so many project ideas fail due to resource constraints or other strategic priorities outside of IT's control.

To combat this reputation, reorient end users to what it takes to say yes to a project. When an organization says yes, it means that there are enough benefits to justify a project, and enough resources to complete the project. It also means that the project's defensible benefits are greater than the benefits of the other projects under review or those already underway. These distinctions are important to understand.

This all sounds reasonable, right? So why do people get so frustrated when they make a request and IT can't automatically say yes? The list of project requests is seemingly bottomless. With finite resources, organizations must say yes to the right projects. It boils down to making choices, just like people do every day with their family budgets and just as we wish Congress would do with the federal budget (if only!).

Task end users to come prepared with new ideas and ready to articulate the benefits of the project. Make sure they get IT Business Partners involved to brainstorm how their ideas might improve decision making, drive efficiencies, improve customer service, or drive more revenue. Re-assigning accountability to end users for requests is a form of project self-selection. It is a subtle but powerful approach that has served me well over the years.

IT Business Partners: Out in Front

IT Business Partners are on the front line in the fight to select the right projects. IT's success depends on staying focused on the right initiatives. Helping end users to self-select wisely is crucial to making this happen. IT Business Partners can help end users understand that their ideas will be fairly weighed against company-wide needs, but that even then, many great ideas still might not win the competition for finite resources. When end users truly understand what it takes to get the green light on a project, they take ownership of IT's yes-or-no decision. This reduces frustration and enhances the reputation of IT as a partner while raising the bar on company performance as a whole. IT Business Partners are crucial in making this happen.

Changing the "IT Is a Bottomless Pit" Perspective

Over the years, I have witnessed many business leaders struggling to understand why IT organizations can't respond quickly to their strategic thoughts and ideas. They have this vague idea that IT is there to enable their business and that anything that will do so should automatically be done. This is the Bottomless Pit perspective: the idea that IT is there to respond to any request at the drop of a hat, or that it has an endless well of resources to draw from. This perspective creates a handful of challenges. Thankfully, a strong IT Business Partnership program usually heads them off.

To start with, executives often fail to hold business leaders accountable for poorly disciplined or incompletely defined strategic plans. This happens when IT investments aren't weighed and vetted in the same way traditional components like competitive factors, marketing, advertising, and staffing are. Business leaders, especially those new in the role, don't think of IT as part of their overall business planning responsibility.

Someone in a sales and marketing leadership role once asked me, "Which IT investments do I need to make to be competitive?" Of course IT has to play a key partnership role in this process, but the question is best answered by understanding what the market dictates in terms of the firm's products and services. In this example, the leader wasn't well versed on the market situation and was struggling to understand how to incorporate IT into her new assignment.

She ultimately decided to engage a third party to collect and analyze market data and customer perceptions of our products and services. This all was organized independently of IT, resulting in a missed opportunity for IT Business Partners to learn firsthand about the company's customers. Our mistake was not introducing our IT Business Partnership program to this new leader early on. Had she known about our collaborative approach from the outset, she could have included us in the process and we would have better understood how to respond.

The Consequences of Un-integrated Plans

If business leaders aren't inspired to strategically collaborate with their IT Business Partners, un-integrated plans, disconnects, and challenges will follow. Even seemingly minor problems can occur when IT is not plugged in from the beginning. This same executive decided to restructure her sales territory. This meant moving people into new roles—promotions, lateral moves, and so forth. The personnel changes were considered top secret. When the restructuring memo came out, the IT organization found out along with the rest of the company, leaving us with only a few weeks to scramble and restructure reporting and sales incentive programs so that they matched the new territories and organizational structure.

Business leaders hadn't thought through the IT implications of their restructuring changes. They erroneously assumed that the reporting and incentive programs would be so easy to adjust that IT barely warranted consideration. To make matters even more challenging, the change happened over a major holiday, requiring a crew of IT business analysts and developers to work over the holiday season. They had to spend time analyzing the impact of the change and reprogramming reports and incentive programs. The executives also asked us to re-report sales histories with both the old and new sales territories. Although this was not a complex technological challenge, the negative impact of so much unanticipated busy work was completely unnecessary.

After the fiasco, we talked with this leader and learned that she'd believed that with all of the IT people we had on board, her changes wouldn't be a big deal to execute. Once she realized the implications to IT and what they had to do to implement her directives, she was empathetic and apologetic. Because she had no perspective on what IT was working on or how resources were prioritized, she believed IT could respond to any request at the drop of a hat, intimating that we were a bottomless pit of resources. Unfortunately, this perspective is all too common among business leaders who often don't understand that IT resources aren't unlimited or interchangeable.

Supply Chain and IT Parallels

To combat the "IT is a bottomless pit" perspective I came across a metaphor that depicts how IT plans operate remarkably like a traditional supply chain. The Supply Chain Council[1] published a high-level model of the components of supply chains that is universally understood by business leaders. What I found most interesting in the model are the parallels to IT project and investment planning. For each stage of the supply chain model, there is a corresponding stage to IT investment planning. The general concepts of the model, such as aligning financial plans, securing resources, and scheduling production, are already well understood and accepted by other business units. Using the model to demonstrate how IT works like the

---

1 The Supply Chain Council was formed in 1996 by PRTM and AMR Research.

supply chain helps business leaders understand what it takes to get things done in IT. The chart below tells the story.

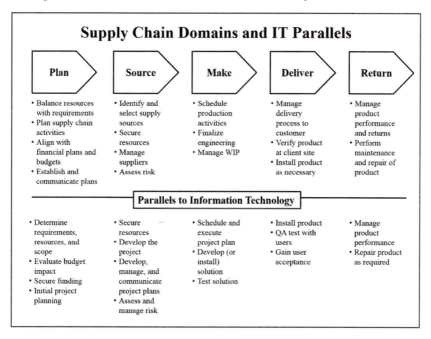

Both teams balance resources and budget impacts during the planning stages of their processes. In the sourcing stage, both teams source raw materials. For the supply chain, this means securing the raw materials to manufacture a product, and for IT this means sourcing the people, hardware, or software required to develop a solution. Both teams develop schedules by which to produce their work and deliver their solutions to the market. The return stage for the supply chain accommodates repairs and corrections; the same is true for IT and its software deployments.

In the early days of our IT Business Partnership program, we struggled to get in sync with our supply chain team. They tended to develop plans independently of IT and had a constantly changing list of project priorities. Once we described the parallels that existed between our two organizations, they saw the wisdom of building integrated plans, thereby reducing the churn of top-priority projects. Our synchronized plans also meant that we were able to complete more high-value projects and drive efficiencies that reduced costs. Our finance and product teams all appreciated the improved results.

Summary:
Elevate Status and Power with Language

Using the language conventions introduced in this chapter will positively impact business outcomes and improve the odds of a successful IT Business Partnership program. Avoid catch phrases like "IT and the business" or "IT and its customers," as this kind of language diminishes IT's role and its ability to positively impact business results. Lead the way and show business leaders how to request and present projects. IT Business Partners can take the emotion out of the process by introducing and reinforcing a more disciplined business approach to project requests. Use the Supply Chain and IT Parallels model as a tool to demonstrate the similarity between traditional supply chain domains and those of IT organizations in a way that business leaders can understand. Overall, the takeaway here is that words shape the perception of IT and impact the success of IT Business Partner programs. Pay attention to the language used inside and outside of IT. You will be surprised at the subtle but powerful impact words have on your program's success.

Chapter Eight

The IT Business Partner's Role in Governance and Strategy

To improve IT's odds of becoming proactively involved in company-wide strategic planning processes, IT must get out of the too-many-projects and too-few-resources game and into a project portfolio investment mindset. IT Business Partners and CIOs that draw on the parallels between financial investments and IT investments can ground executive thinking. Executives understand that not all financial investments are safe: some are riskier and some have a higher ROI, just like IT investments. Drawing on these similarities elevates the topic of IT investments and puts them on a level playing field with all the other company investments.

Business leaders are familiar with investment decision trade-offs. They routinely make them all year long, especially during the annual budget process. They consider whether marketing should invest in additional research or if a large capital investment should be made in R&D, or in a factory, or in brick-and-mortar stores. Similarly, IT investments must be included in this same conversation.

IT Business Partners must be actively involved in developing investment Business Cases. They need to understand the start-up costs, ongoing costs, and the benefits of investments. They also need to understand the market impacts of an investment decision and conversely, the ramifications of not moving forward on a particular investment. The more they know about Business Case levers, the more their knowledge will be valued throughout the organization. IT Business Partners who spend time in the field with customers can personalize their stories and relate real customer interactions when pitching investments to management. Business leaders absolutely love it when IT takes a strong role in selling their ideas internally. It makes them feel like they aren't facing the world alone. Of course, ultimately they are still accountable for the investment, but having a strong IT Business Partner makes their job a lot easier.

Business Investment Governance

Companies are becoming more familiar with the concept of IT governance. In fact, IT research bodies such as Gartner and Forrester have been writing about the virtues of IT governance for some time now. Having implemented the process for a number of companies, I can vouch for the benefits of IT governance programs, though getting the executive team involved is tough to do. However, once there, they see value in the process and are able to better connect IT performance to company performance. The challenge is getting executives to the discussion table and then making the process meaningful for them.

RENAMING IT GOVERNANCE

There is a clear movement in the industry to get away from the more formal and, some say, antiquated title of "IT governance." I am in that camp and prefer to use the term "Business Technology Investment Committee" or just "Business Investment Committee." Forrester has taken this concept one step further and now refers to IT as BT, as in business technology. This reinforces the notion that IT organizations contribute greatly to the company's strategic progress and market results.

I applaud the change. In fact, a couple of years ago I made a New Year's resolution to never again utter the phrase "IT and the business." One of the ways I made this a lasting change was by dropping the term "IT governance" and instead adapting the BT acronym in my everyday communications. "The Business Technology Investment Committee" feels like a bit of a mouthful at first, but business leaders quickly get in the habit of referring to BTIC (pronounced *b-tick*).

BTIC OWNERSHIP

Many IT organizations are initially challenged with how to run a BTIC meeting: Who from the IT organization should participate? Who from executive management should attend? How often should the meetings occur? Who should present at them? Conflicts surface between the PMO and IT Business Partners as to who should host or drive BTIC meetings. Both teams want to own the process, and both think that they are the natural leaders of the meetings. In truth, both organizations play important roles in the process. IT Business Partners represent their business unit's processes, customers, and priorities. The PMO provides insight into the current portfolio of projects and resource-planning activities related to the active portfolio. A framework for BTIC roles and responsibilities is detailed below.

THE PURPOSE OF GOVERNANCE

It is important to establish the purpose of any business process. I favor a simple and straightforward approach because anything more complex tends to support the notion that whatever IT touches becomes overly complicated.

There are generally only four reasons to organize investment committees:

1. *To provide strategic leadership and investment congruence*
   Investment committees provide strategic leadership for business technology investments by matching new investment opportunities with enterprise strategic objectives and processes.

2. *To prioritize new and existing investments*
   Investment committees prioritize business technology investment initiatives and deliver final approvals and recommendations regarding proposed business technology projects.

3. *To track existing business technology investments*
   Investment committees provide management oversight and guidance on active business technology investments to ensure accountability and results.

4. *To communicate investment decisions*
   Investment committees ensure investment decision transparency and promote collaboration and understanding across all functional units.

Ideally, committee team members represent the executive leadership team, the CIO, the IT Business Partners, the PMO director, and someone from financial management (usually the CFO). You might have more attendees, of course, and they can actively participate in the dialogue, but they should not have voting privileges. Voting on investments should be the sole responsibility of the executive team.

Additional non-voting team members might include the enterprise risk management team, if the company has this function, or business unit financial analysts (this could be agenda-specific). See the following page for a quick summary of the key functional roles.

When examining new investments and reporting on active projects, provide a framework to show where they are along the path. For this purpose, utilizing a stage-gate process is effective. For many

BTIC Roles Grid

Area	Role	Responsibility
Executive Committee Members	• Strategic vision & oversight	• Business & market alignment • Overall investment oversight • Risk/return oversight • Constituent communications/portfolio transparency/business accountability
CIO	• IIT oversight • Holistic planning • Governance	• BTIC meeting owner • Strategic planning & business alignment • Investment budget oversight • Business-results-oriented reporting
IT Business Partners	• Business unit advocate • Customer advocate	• Business unit alignment • Business case formulation • Roadmap positioning
PMO	• Project tracking • Project management • Resource planning	• Project execution & risk management • Scope management • Project financial management
Financial Management	• Financial oversight • Financial savvy	• Asset allocation • Financial tracking • Spending oversight

business executives, the concept of stage gates is new. I use the simple six-phase stage-gate process below to show management where initiatives are in the process.

Investment Stage Gates

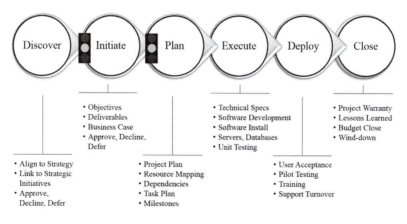

Discover • Initiate • Plan • Execute • Deploy • Close

• Objectives
• Deliverables
• Business Case
• Approve, Decline, Defer

• Technical Specs
• Software Development
• Software Install
• Servers, Databases
• Unit Testing

• Project Warranty
• Lessons Learned
• Budget Close
• Wind-down

• Align to Strategy
• Link to Strategic Initiatives
• Approve, Decline, Defer

• Project Plan
• Resource Mapping
• Dependencies
• Task Plan
• Milestones

• User Acceptance
• Pilot Testing
• Training
• Support Turnover

Investment Stage Gates

Generally, the first two gates, Discover and Initiate, deal with go/no-go decisions from the BTIC. IT Business Partners should be actively involved in these phases. They should either drive, or at the very least be actively involved in Business Case development. The PMO takes over at the planning phase and then drives the execution of the active projects.

THE DISCOVER STAGE GATE

The primary focus of the Discover stage gate should be:

1. **Align** to company strategy
2. **Prioritize** a gut check for new investments
3. **Perform** an impact assessment of adding new investments to the current project portfolio

These factors get executive teams thinking about whether an investment should be pursued. The investment-decision options at this gate are:

1. **Approve** the investment for progression to the Initiation stage gate
2. **Defer** the investment decision to a later date
3. **Decline** approval of the investment

THE INITIATION STAGE GATE

During the Initiation stage gate, the focus is on determining business requirements, costs, and benefits. Develop a project charter that spells out the deliverables of the project and any items that won't be tackled during the effort if approved. During this phase, a financial analysis is developed along with a corresponding Business Case. The investment-decision options at this stage gate are:

1. **Approve** the investment to the Plan stage gate

2. *Defer* the investment decision to a later date

3. *Decline* approval to move forward with the investment

KEEPING INVESTMENT-DECISION CRITERIA SIMPLE

When considering investments, bear in mind that investment decisions generally fall into one of the three decision criteria:

1. They drive top-line revenue

2. They drive bottom-line savings

3. They mitigate risk (compliance)

You could add a fourth criterion that focuses on strategic fit, but generally this is addressed by the investment's cost/benefit.

Size Matters: Tailoring Your Governance Process

Governance processes must be tailored to each organization. Cultural factors are shaped by the size of the company, whether it is private or public, and by the appetite business leaders have for process in general. Regardless of these factors, keep it simple. Take your governance process for a test drive. Preview investments with members of the IT organization first, and then with the leadership team. Make sure that any leadership preview sessions, which are essentially preselling, are conducted privately, one-on-one. Giving executives an intimate preview lets them safely voice their concerns and suggestions without the pressure of dissenting opinions from louder, more vocal team members in group sessions.

Operational Projects and Governance

Determine the size and scale of projects that will go through the BTIC process. Smaller-scale initiatives, typically operational projects, won't usually warrant as much decision and execution rigor as large-scale investments do. Demand for operational projects typically surfaces during the fiscal year. It would be nice if all projects for the portfolio, regardless of scale, could be considered during the annual planning process. Unfortunately, this isn't realistic. Operational teams have to respond to events in real time because the market factors that drive potential investments don't always fit neatly into the annual budget process.

Process Considerations for Operational Projects

There are a number of key characteristics to consider when designing your operational project's business process:

1. **Engaged.** IT Business Partners need to be engaged in handling demand management for operational projects.
2. **Responsive.** The IT organization must be perceived as being responsive, flexible, and adaptive when they address operational project demand.
3. **Transparent.** Executive management must be kept up-to-date on which operational projects are being undertaken and completed.
4. **Oversight.** The PMO must skillfully execute operational projects and provide the appropriate level of project oversight to ensure their success.

An Organization Model for Operational Projects

Developing an organization model that is responsive to tactical requests tamps down the "Department of No" reputation of IT organizations. I like to create two operational teams dedicated to working on tactical initiatives. One team focuses on small-scale initiatives that generally don't involve capital spending and whose duration is less than a quarter. The other team focuses on reporting and data-related requests.

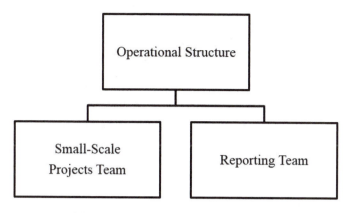

Operational Initiatives Structure

Operational projects don't require the full PMO treatment to manage them, but they do require oversight and need to be part of the governance process. Because they are small, don't burden the executive team with making decisions about which operational projects to undertake. The decision processes and tools used to manage operational projects are discussed in detail in chapter nine. However, because operational projects are a part of governance, a brief explanation of their integration into the BTIC process is necessary here.

OPERATIONAL PROJECTS:
A HIGH-LEVEL PROCESS OVERVIEW

It is a good idea to give the process a name that doesn't immediately awaken the yawn reflex in your leadership team. Calling it the "Operational Projects Process" is likely to do just that. One clever analyst I worked with came up with the name "Quarterly Sprints." I like the name because it sounds zippy and sends a responsive message.

Quarterly Sprint projects were prioritized by IT Business Partners and the IT leadership team. The IT Business Partners collected tactical project ideas during a given quarter. One month before the beginning of each new quarter the IT Business Partners organized a priority-setting exercise in which IT leaders participated. The collected ideas were vetted and ranked during this meeting.

Then our PMO took the prioritized list and mapped any resources needed to execute the projects, starting with the highest priority project on the list. Items that didn't make the list due to resource constraints were deferred or cancelled. The list became the proposed set of operational projects that we recommended moving ahead with in the next quarter.

As CIO, I was an active participant in this process. We reviewed the results of our prioritization at monthly BTIC meetings and asked for management approval. Typically this was a quick review, usually with little or no discussion. Because we showed our work, the executives could easily see the ranked projects and understood why some projects didn't get staffed. We then asked the BTIC members for their approval; once we had it, we knew our tactical initiatives for the next 90 days.

There was a side benefit of moving to the quarterly process. We used to meet each week to review operational projects and resource utilization. The Quarterly Sprint process reduced the actual time we spent on this process by over 75 percent. Occasionally there were project needs that surfaced between sprints, but they became the exception rather than the rule.

Completed Projects: Value Delivered

We shared completed strategic and operational projects monthly as part of our standing "value delivered" section of the governance process. Executives enjoyed seeing the completed projects. For some, this was the only exposure they had to initiatives outside of their specific area of responsibility. I like to see completed projects presented directly after the agenda review. It sets a nice positive tone for the remainder of the meeting.

Some CIOs I talk to omit this important step in the process. But sharing successes isn't bragging or self-promoting if done subtly. Organizations make significant investments in people and technology, and sharing the results of completed projects should be a given. In the case of my own company, we typically share only highlights of completed projects. We describe the resulting business impact of the investment in terms that the executives understand. Skipping this step ensures that a vital benefit of the governance process will be missed. IT Business Partners are best positioned to highlight these results because they know the customers and the challenges better than anyone in the organization.

When to Use Policies to Manage the Governance Process

Business committees like the BTIC tend to drive the need for more formal documentation. It is a good idea to write a policy statement that provides official guardrails for the process. Regardless of whether your organization develops a policy, IT Business Partners must be at the front line of all requests. To make sure the organization follows this principle, consider eliminating all formal request forms. Encourage and eventually require anyone who wants to request a project to see their IT Business Partner in person. Doing so positions IT Business Partners to drive the formal process and encourages collaboration with business units to capture the relevant project vetting information.

If you do decide to build a policy for BTIC, don't over-think or over-engineer it. Keep it simple. Use the following grids to determine where to draw the line on requiring a formal Business Case, financial analysis, or presentation to the BTIC. Be sure to fine-tune financial thresholds to fit with the company spending policies.

Budgeted Investments				
From	To	Business Case	Financial Analysis	Presentation
$0	$24,999			
$25,000	$124,999	√		
$125,000	$199,999	√		√
$200,000	> $200,000	√	√	√

Unbudgeted Investments				
From	To	Business Case	Financial Analysis	Presentation
$0	$9,999			
$10,000	$49,999	√		
$50,000	$99,999	√		√
$100,000	> $100,000	√	√	√

Summary: Process Brings Order and Transparency

Using the BTIC process gets IT off the reactionary project roller-coaster ride that often occurs in companies. IT Business Partners are well positioned to drive the BTIC process, especially through the Discovery and Initiation stages. Ultimately, governance doesn't have to be a dirty word. Instead, when handled well, the whole process can bring welcome clarity to decisions and visibility to the management team. I encourage you to share decision results with the entire organization. Transparency legitimizes the business process, and has the added benefit of helping people around the company understand what is being approved and what has management's attention. It will also give enterprising and aspiring leaders a framework to engage with management and IT on important investments they want to champion.

IT Business Partners have a real opportunity to earn their stripes via a well-executed BTIC process. The more often valued ideas get launched and successfully executed, the more trust and respect is earned by IT. No single thing can influence IT's reputation more than getting projects approved and done right. This requires a real partnership with the business, and it requires a well-coordinated effort between the IT Business Partners and the PMO.

When IT organizations eliminate the process mystery, end users take ownership and become more engaged in the investment process. There are three areas IT Business Partners and the IT organization can focus on in particular to increase end user engagement and transparency:

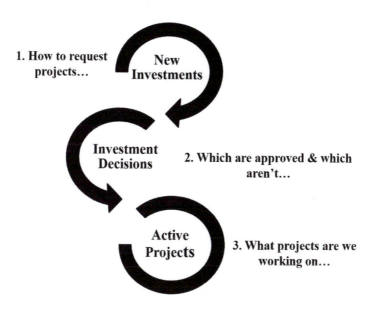

1. How to request projects...

New Investments

Investment Decisions

2. Which are approved & which aren't...

Active Projects

3. What projects are we working on...

The Steps to Achieving IT Transparency

1. How projects are requested (there is more on this topic in chapter nine)

2. How investment decisions are made

3. What projects IT is working on (there is more on this topic in chapter fifteen)

All three demystify the process and help end users see IT as a peer and trusted advisor.

Chapter Nine

IT Business Partners and the Project Management Office

When I launched my first IT Business Partnership program years ago, a tug-of-war erupted around who was in charge of the PMO intake process. The same thing happened later at successive companies. The dilemma was always whether it should be owned by the PMO director or the IT Business Partner. I have since had many one-on-one discussions with members of both teams, each camp articulately stating their case for ownership. In actuality, ownership of the process falls into two distinct areas of responsibility. The first deals with accountability relating to ideas and getting them vetted. The second deals with the actual business processes that guide the vetting process.

Determining Areas of Responsibility

IT Business Partners are responsible for getting ideas into the intake process. They are charged with understanding the needs of their business unit, its customers, and market priorities. Ideas come from many sources and directions including sales team members, competitors, customers, operations teams, and the company's strategic plans. Armed with an intimate knowledge of the challenges and opportunities facing the business unit, IT Business Partners are best qualified to bring ideas to the table. They bear frontline responsibility, but in a carefully orchestrated fashion with the PMO.

The PMO director is responsible for the mechanics that govern the intake process. They are charged with making sure that a consistent, easy-to-use process is followed, giving visibility to ideas across the organization. They are also responsible for facilitating the scoring and analysis of candidate projects in the intake process. In addition, the PMO performs a preliminary analysis of the necessary resources to execute new projects. They also review the impact potential projects might have on the active project portfolio, the budget, and required resource levels. And finally, once business technology investments are given the green light, the PMO makes sure projects are effectively planned and executed.

INTAKE COLLABORATION IS CRUCIAL

Both the PMO and IT Business Partner teams must collaborate. This is especially true when looking at investment ideas from across the company. Both teams must take a wide-reaching, corporate perspective. IT Business Partners have to strongly represent their business units, but more significantly, they have to think corporately and put company-wide priorities first. At times there will be projects they are particularly passionate about, even though they know another business unit's project must take priority. In these instances, it is helpful to treat the investments as though you are spending your own money. When an IT Business Partner struggles to maintain a truly corporate perspective, the CIO will need to step in to ensure that this view takes precedence.

FOSTER HEALTHY DEBATE

As teams collaborate on the intake process, it is important to create an environment where healthy debate takes place. Living in Minnesota for a number of years, I have learned much about "Minnesota Nice."

This tendency toward passive-aggressiveness is a cultural trademark of the state, and there is some truth to the statement that if passive-aggression were an Olympic sport, Minnesota would dominate. However, regardless of what state or country you are from, you have to have a healthy debate of ideas. It is destructive to IT's inner group dynamics and reputation if they allow investment decisions to be vetted without good debate.

Hold Each Other Accountable

With resources and investment dollars in short supply, passions regarding business technology investments run deep. There is no doubt that someone will leave an intake vetting process unhappy with its outcome. IT has to be unified and supportive once an agreement is made. Team members who voice their unhappiness with the final intake decision need to be called back into line. Such unsupportive behavior feeds negative business unit perceptions of IT. Instead, team members need to make sure that their passion is on the table during the vetting process. A healthy debate will drive better, more informed decision making. The whole process is quickly undermined when business units hear disgruntled IT team members complain about a particular idea being rejected.

One way to take emotion out of the equation is to build a structured investment process. As discussed in chapter seven, it is never fun to tell an end user that their idea didn't make the grade. IT Business Partners, or anyone in IT for that matter, should have an intelligent conversation with a project sponsor about why their investment idea didn't make the cut or how their Business Case could be beefed up if they want it to come back around in the future.

Building an Intake Process Framework

Building an intake process framework requires collaboration within the IT organization and with the IT Business Partner's support. The process should leverage the strategic imperatives and goals established by the executive leadership team. Each investment idea that surfaces must be measured in a logical and consistent way that makes sense to business leaders. The process must be simple, but getting it there takes time and effort. Leonardo da Vinci put it well when he said, "Simplicity is the ultimate sophistication."

TWO INVESTMENT PATHS

Investments typically follow either a strategic or operational path. Investments on the strategic path are usually developed as part of a company's annual budget process. Operational projects, on the other hand, can surface at any time during the fiscal year. In general, projects that are considered during the annual budget process are larger in scope and require larger capital expenditures. These investments are typically a critical part of a company's strategic plan and frequently come freshly squeezed as part of the executive team's last planning retreat. Operational projects are typically driven by a newly discovered operational challenge, a new customer opportunity, or a new risk-related event. Regardless of the path, rigor is required to properly evaluate and prioritize both strategic and operational ideas.

LEVERAGE ROADMAPS IN THE BUDGET PROCESS

If your company is like many, the annual planning process can be quite cumbersome. And, if yours is like two-thirds of the companies Forrester Research points out, IT is usually not in the loop during the planning process. This is a critical area where IT Business Partners can make an impactful difference. As part of their overall responsibilities, IT Business Partners develop investment roadmaps for their business units. The investments under consideration as part of the annual process should be taken directly from IT Business Partner roadmaps.

IT Business Partners must effectively communicate their business unit's investment roadmap to their business unit's leadership team, the IT organization, and executive management. The annual budget process is greatly simplified when the roadmaps are well understood and utilized, and there will be fewer surprises not only for the IT organization, but for all those involved in the budget planning process. In fact, CFOs like to integrate these investment roadmaps when updating the company's long-range financial plans.

Operational Projects Dominate Time and Attention

Strategic projects typically get all the headlines and management attention. For IT Business Partners, however, the reality is that operational projects demand much of their time. The volume of operational requests is significantly higher than strategic projects, and the urgency of daily operations requires that new items get vetted often. This strains not only IT Business Partners but also IT resource managers, the PMO, and most of all the IT organization. Every IT organization is faced with this challenge.

There are many ways to tackle the demand management challenge we face in IT organizations. One approach that I am particularly fond of was developed as part of an overall PMO tune-up effort we undertook. The premise of the approach assumed that operational requests would continue to arrive in the intake process and that to maintain strong working relationships with operational units, IT had to respond to these requests in a fair and equitable way.

Prior to our new process, we spent an inordinate amount of time prioritizing and reprioritizing projects, conducting resource assessments, and re-planning our work. Typically, IT organizations do this on a weekly or monthly basis. We decided to shift our operational project focus to quarterly windows. This meant that in order to be considered, operational projects had to be small enough to be completed within a three-month timeframe so as to fit into our Quarterly Sprint process.

Quarterly Sprint Tools

We used specific tools to manage the Quarterly Sprint process. First, we would cover the intake process with the 1-Pager tool to capture requirements and benefits for operational projects. Then, we would detail the process flow, decision tools, and management communication techniques.

THE 1-PAGER

One of the useful tools my teams developed to capture investment opportunities was a one-page form that we creatively called the 1-Pager. Not intended to replace a full-blown Business Case, the 1-Pager was simply used as a framework to encourage discussion. IT Business Partners drove the process of populating the form's information. I had used the same high-level information to drive the decision process for strategic and operational projects. The form was organized in the following manner:

Section One: Project Overview

This section should include the most basic information: the date the idea was captured, the name of the project, the type of project (strategic, operational, break-fix, etc.), the business sponsor, and a brief description of the project.

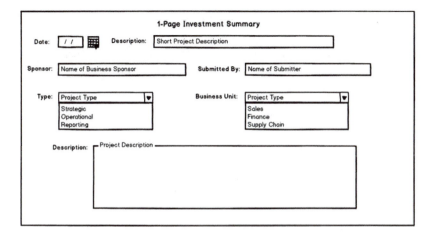

Section Two: Justification

This aspect of the 1-Pager describes the high-level benefits of the investment and captures how the investment aligns to the company's strategic objectives. To make this effective, work with the executive team to get agreement on what these objectives should be. Examples include extending brand reach or reaching certain growth or market share objectives. It is also helpful to capture the degree to which the investment aligns to these goals. I have used a five-scale system in the past with a rating that ranges from 5 for completely aligned down to 1, indicating limited alignment. Consider including a short description of why the investment aligns and how the success of the project will be measured.

We also captured justification drivers: Does the investment drive new revenue, save money, or address a compliance requirement?

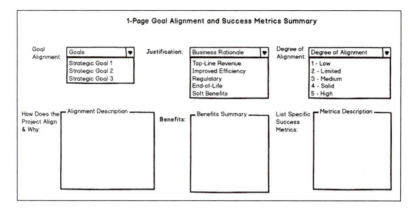

Section Three: Dependencies and Workarounds

This section describes project dependencies; in other words, actions that must be completed or resources that must be secured before the requested project can be achieved. Known workarounds should be documented because they are likely to be a driver for the investment in the first place.

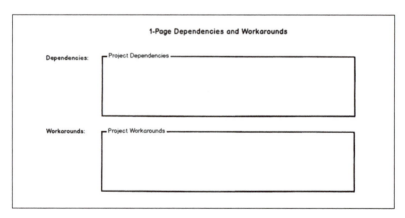

Section Four: Benefits

This section captures the hard benefits you expect will be realized by the project. I include a range of cost savings or new revenues as a placeholder for the investment. It might even be useful to capture soft benefits such as improved morale or improved job satisfaction. These typically don't have a major role in getting an investment funded, but including them demonstrates dimension and thoroughness of thought to the overall investment idea.

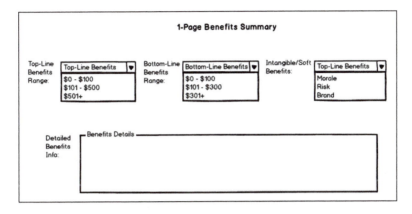

Section Five: Resources

Use this section to list the needed resources estimated to execute the project. This includes both IT resources as well as resources from other business units. Additionally, capture any known incremental project costs including hardware, software, and consulting or service costs. People, hardware, and software all contribute to the total cost of completing a project.

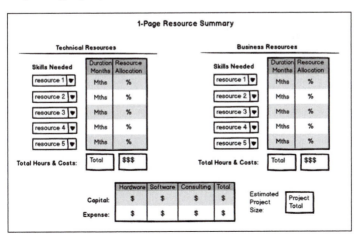

Section Six: Decision

The final section is reserved as a place to record the outcome of the investment's "go/no-go" decision process.

1-Page Business Technology Investment Committee Decision
PMO Administration
Date Presented: [/ /] 🔢   ☐ Approve   ☐ Defer   ☐ Decline

FORM DEFINITIONS

The following is a brief summary of the field definitions you should use to develop the 1-Pager form. Be sure to tailor this form to your company's processes and policies.

Data Field	Description
Date	Use today's date
Project Name	This name will be used for status reporting and resource assignment.
Project Type	Generally strategic or operational. Strategic projects are those where the project cost exceeds $100k and/or requires more than 1,000 resource hours.
Business Unit	The area that is requesting this project.
Submitted By	The person who prepares the form and can speak about it at BTIC meetings.
Business Sponsor	Generally the business person who sees the need for the change and has the authority to make it happen.
Project Description	A brief description of the work that needs to be done. Include any relevant background for the audience to understand why the work is being requested. If possible, identify systems that might need to be reviewed or changed.
Alignment to Corporate Goals	Which corporate goals does this project support? If more than one goal is met, pick the primary goal that it supports.
Degree of Alignment	How strongly (on a 1-5 scale) does this project impact the achievement of the corporate goal that was chosen?
How Does It Align &Why?	Fill out to support the degree of alignment to corporate goals that were chosen.
What Success Metrics Will We Use?	What metrics will measure how much this project "moved the needle" on supporting the corporate goal?
Operational Justification	List operational reasons not articulated by the corporate goals which support the reason for undertaking the project.
Other Justification	This field can be used when a project is requested due to regulatory, legal, or end-of-life issues.
Upstream/Downstream Dependencies or Considerations	List any projects or work that need to be completed prior to this project being started or any other projects or initiatives that are dependent upon this work being completed.
Available Workaround	Describe other ways to solve the problem this project proposes to resolve.
Estimated Benefits – Hard	Choose the level of top-line or bottom-line benefits likely to be realized from this project's implementation. If there are no quantifiable benefits, choose the option labeled "none, soft benefits only."

The 1-Pager is flexible enough to use for annual project vetting and operational (Quarterly Sprint) vetting. The process is simple and doesn't bog down executive teams with the particular details of tactical projects.

Quarterly Sprint Process Flow

Here is a high-level summary of how the Quarterly Sprint process works:

1. IT Business Partners collect project ideas during the quarter.
2. We then populate 1-Pagers for those tactical projects we intend to prioritize and vet in the upcoming quarter.
3. IT resource managers review the 1-Pagers to confirm resource needs for each project.
4. The IT leadership team meets to review the 1-Pagers one month prior to the beginning of the next quarter. IT Business Partners lead a high-level overview of each project. All participants are required to read the 1-Pagers prior to meeting so that the focus is on answering questions and debating the merits of candidate projects.
5. The IT leadership team members score and rank the projects, and the PMO director compiles the results.
6. The prioritized list is reviewed. In a separate exercise, the PMO team assigns resources to projects until all available resources are fully utilized.
7. The list of staffed resources is reviewed by IT leadership one last time; adjustments and confirmations are made.
8. The final list is presented to the BTIC for approval.
9. BTIC decisions are announced to IT and the rest of the company.
10. Work commences on the list at the beginning of the next quarter.

Scoring Criteria

During our IT leadership meetings, an additional set of criteria is examined as a way to vet the candidate Quarterly Sprint projects. We explore six additional criteria to put the projects in priority order (each can have a value from 1-5):

Scoring Criteria	Description	Weight
1. Strategic Fit	• How well does the candidate project fit with strategic goals?	20%
2. Operational Fit	• Does the project address a key operational pain point?	20%
3. End-of-Life	• Does the project address a system end-of-life issue?	20%
4. Cost/Benefit	• How attractive is the cost benefit of the project?	20%
5. Risk	• Is the project likely to be successful if undertaken?	10%
6. Cost Certainty	• Are project costs and duration well understood?	10%

Sample Aggregate Voting Results

The aggregate voting results show each investment candidate ranked by scoring results. This makes it easy to see which projects have the most and least business impact. Use this information to explain which projects make or don't make the cut.

Rank	Score	Projects	Staffed	Start	End
1	100.00	Upgrade Executive Metrics	Yes	Jul-13	Sep-13
2	94.67	Upgrade Manufacturing Server	Yes	Jul-13	Sep-13
3	75.56	Enhance Order Management	Yes	Jul-13	Aug-13
4	75.56	Enhance Demand Planning Reporting	Yes	Jul-13	Sep-13
5	69.78	On-boarding Workflow Update	Yes	Aug-13	Sep-13
6	66.67	DR Server / Data Moves	Yes	Aug-13	Sep-13
7	58.00	Budget System Upgrade	No		

Rank	Score	Projects	Staffed	Start	End
8	56.22	Cost Accounting Upgrade	No		
9	54.44	AP Automation - Discovery	No		
10	54.00	Time & Attendance Upgrade	No		

Sample Scoring Sheet

The scoring tool is used to record candidate investment alignment with the six scoring criteria mentioned above. The example below reflects the aggregate scoring results for each candidate project by scoring criteria. This information provides insight into how the scores were determined for each investment.

Scoring Results: Quarterly BTIC Meeting							
Score projects on a scale of 1 - 5	Alignment to strategic goals	Addresses key operational issue or pain point	Addresses end-of-life issues	Attractiveness of cost/benefit	Project Risk Profile (1 = most risky)	Certainty of project costs & duration	
Weighting	20%	20%	20%	20%	10%	10%	
Modification to Order Management	2.33	3.33	1.33	3.67	4.11	3.67	58.22
AP Automation - Discovery	2.11	3.56	1.11	2.78	4.44	3.67	54.44
Automate Retail Standard Cost	2.78	3.78	1.11	2.56	4.11	3.56	56.22
Financial / Bank Reconciliation Tool	2.89	3.44	1.00	2.67	3.56	3.44	54.00
Sales Portal Upgrade	1.56	2.89	4.22	2.78	3.33	2.78	58.00

Once the Quarterly Sprint process becomes more broadly known in the organization, the number of drive-by requests will shrink. These are the ad-hoc hallway pleas from just about anyone hoping to get ideas prioritized outside of the official vetting process. You can never eliminate them totally, but when they do occur, simply point people to their designated IT Business Partner.

Quarterly Sprints become a tactical pressure release valve, so consider ramping up the team size to match your company's appetite for these types of projects. When they are struggling financially, companies tend to pull back on strategic projects, temporarily making operational projects IT's top priority. When operational projects are done well, end user satisfaction rises, and this can be used later to secure funding for strategic initiatives when the business climate rebounds.

Summary: Build Trust through Effective Project Intake Management

Managing the intake process is a full-time job for IT Business Partners. They are best positioned to handle new requests because they are closest to customers and spend time in the field observing customer interactions with company tools. Collaboration between the PMO and IT Business Partners is crucial when balancing the influx of great ideas and the realities of limited resources. There are always more investment ideas than there are company resources to execute them. The BTIC process framework provides a consistent way for vetting new investment ideas.

Managing the strategic initiative intake process is less volatile than managing the intake process for operational projects. By their nature, operational projects are hard to predict and plan for. The 1-Pager and Quarterly Sprint process offer a safety valve to take the pressure off the endless supply of operational projects. Keep things simple to ensure that end users don't become intimidated by the process.

The BTIC and Quarterly Sprint approaches bring clarity and consistency to what can be an emotional process for end users. End users appreciate the rigor and predictability that these processes deliver, and these processes create trust between the IT organization and partner business units.

Chapter Ten

IT Business Partner Tools

Linking business technology projects to business goals is a chief responsibility of the IT Business Partner. A toolkit that clearly communicates priorities and plans to business unit leaders and employees is crucial to their success. The tools referenced in this chapter are based on what I've used in the past as a former product manager and as a manager of product managers. I draw from the Product Development Management Association (PDMA) and its wealth of knowledge and expertise relating to the processes needed to build market-savvy product solutions.

Many of the tools that product managers use can be effectively leveraged by IT Business Partners as they develop multi-year plans and roadmaps for their business units. The skills acquired through the PDMA are essentially just fundamental business skills. Today, there aren't specific certifications available for the IT Business Partner role in the same way there are for other IT skills, such as the PMI certification for project managers. From a career development perspective, I have asked enterprising IT Business Partner candidates to seek formal PDMA training in the form of the New Product Development Professional (NPDP) certification.

Driving Market Value

While there may not be a one-to-one link between managing a product and partnering with a business unit, both roles focus on driving value in market terms. IT Business Partners need to understand the market concerns of their business units. If they are managing internal groups such as HR, finance, or supply chain teams, it can be difficult initially to directly connect their priorities to the marketplace, though the connections are indeed there. For HR, it could be that a competitor is perceived as a better place to work. For example, the competitor might have better training programs or on-boarding tools. If the focus is on supply chain, competitors might have an advantage in fulfillment or multichannel commerce. In the finance area, competitors could have more innovative business insight tools that help business developers respond proactively to market trends. Every business unit has a connection to the market. These groups don't exist just to exist; they are there to help companies serve customers and compete more effectively.

Working with Product Managers

If your company sells products or services, it is quite likely that someone is performing the Product Manager role whether or not this is their official title. Additionally, your company might have Digital Product Managers (sometimes called Web Product Managers), which have recently surged in popularity at companies selling their products through digital channels. This is good news, as IT Business Partners can learn a lot from these groups. IT Business Partners in these companies might not be accountable for gathering competitive information, but it is their responsibility to understand the market and how it impacts their business unit. Without this understanding, IT will have difficulty driving business value.

Forming close business relationships with existing product management teams connects the dots between business priorities and solutions. Determining how these groups will integrate processes is crucial if you are to avoid an IT Business Partner role that relies solely on antiquated, less effective handoffs. This means ensuring the IT Business Partners have an opportunity to meet with customers, participate in field research, and to collaborate on roadmap development. This takes thoughtful consideration, and mapping this all out early on in the process will avoid role confusion and staff frustration later on.

There are three tools that I will discuss in this chapter: the Capabilities (Product) Plan, the Release Plan, and Roadmaps. As with all the processes and tools presented in this book, you will need to tailor these to the particular characteristics of your company. Keep it simple. You don't have to use every idea outlined here. Adopt a crawl-walk-run approach when introducing these tools. Introducing too much process too soon can overwhelm and stifle your business units.

The Capability Plan (a.k.a. The Product Plan)

The Capability Plan concept is loosely modeled on the PDMA's product plan. The term "Capability Plan" is apt because most business units won't have a product that needs managing, per se. This is especially true when it comes to internal business units such as finance or HR. Frankly, it doesn't matter much what it is called—what does matter is understanding the purpose behind the plan and how IT Business Partners should use it. Let's start with a high-level definition of the Capability Plan:

> **The Capability Plan:** The Capability Plan is used to define the overall vision and strategic direction for a business

unit. It is intended to describe the business unit capabilities, business processes, key attributes, targeted roadmap, competitive strengths, market opportunities, strategic alignment, high-level resources, and financial parameters.

Essentially, the Capability Plan is a tool used to define a collection of new business unit capabilities required to achieve critical business objectives. An excellent example of how this applies comes from the accounting industry. While CIO at a top-five accounting firm, I had a corporate initiative to achieve 15 percent revenue growth in one of our core business lines. Our IT Business Partner in this business unit had a few key IT capabilities in mind that needed to be addressed if we were to achieve these growth goals.

Working with the business unit, we developed a plan that outlined our approach to enable the growth goals. We knew that our company's tools were lacking and staff turnover was higher than the industry average, and our firm's goal was to grow both organically and through acquisition. We also knew that we needed to strategically address the tools and business technology constraints of the current systems if we were to have any hope of achieving these goals.

To that end, we developed a Capability Plan that addressed several critical gaps. The gaps included:

1. An inability to move work from office to office: Staffing levels and business activity varied from one location to another. The firm had no easy way to move work around their more than 100 offices short of using FedEx or UPS to physically move documents between locations; not a terribly efficient or secure way to conduct business.

2. A lack of standard methods: Much of the work performed by this group was manual. This resulted in each office using a different method to complete the same work. When we asked about

standards; one partner responded by saying, "Yes, we have standards, each office has their own." That comment still makes me smile to this day. If we were going to share work across offices, we knew we had to introduce a standardized toolset.

3. A heavy reliance on paper: Without tools, the only way to perform billable work was with the original customer documents. Too much time was spent looking for client paperwork or just waiting for it to arrive via courier. This constraint would need to be eliminated if we were to have a chance at meeting our growth goals.

Our resulting Capabilities Plan was focused on the approach needed to overcome these obstacles. Our plan outlined the technical solutions we believed would address the challenges we uncovered during our field research efforts. As discussed in chapter five, seeing is believing. This research was instrumental in helping us build our overall plan for this group. Our Capabilities Plan contained the following twelve elements:

1. **Executive Summary:** We described the objectives of the plan, gave a background on the current situation, and summarized the issues revealed by the field research.

2. **Targeted Audience:** In this section we described the audience that would benefit from the capabilities outlined in our plan, including the more than 2,000 tax employees needed to support the planned business growth.

3. **Competitive Analysis:** This included a brief summary of our competitors. We outlined what their tools and capabilities were versus our own tools, and we captured quotes from tax professionals with experience at other firms. We also highlighted the firm's historically slow pace at adapting technology as a barrier to hiring new talent.

4. **Capability Objectives:** This section described our objectives for the initiatives outlined in the overall strategic plan. We talked about enabling a more mobile workforce, increasing staff efficiency, delivering better oversight and transparency of work in process, and improving employee engagement and morale.

5. **Strengths and Weaknesses:** Here we outlined employee technology adoption challenges and described third-party solution providers' market strengths (or lack thereof).

6. **Capabilities Plan and Strategy:** This is where we described the capabilities we wanted to address to achieve the stated business goals. In this example, we talked about document imaging and scanning and workflow tools. We talked about how we would package the capabilities into logical solution themes. We documented the priority for each theme area that drove our Capability Roadmap.

7. **Capabilities Roadmap:** This visual tool reflects the themes outlined in the strategy section above. We documented the key capabilities that fell under each theme, and we used calendar quarters to reflect anticipated implementation timeframes that matched our priorities. If we had used specific dates instead of quarters, it would have implied a level of accuracy that wasn't realistic until funding and project plans were in place.

8. **Alignment:** This section highlighted how the capabilities described in the plan connected to the firm's overall strategic imperatives.

9. **Technology Overview:** Here we documented a high-level technology plan that we intended to use to execute the points outlined in the strategy. We also used this section to highlight any new skills IT might need to introduce these new technologies to our employees.

10. **Trends:** This section detailed macro industry trends that could potentially impact the company or business units. This is where you would include information about trends in leveraging offshore resources, e-commerce solution proliferation, cloud computing, baby-boomer retirements, and so forth. We included any relevant facts that added color and dimension to the plan.

11. **Assumptions:** We documented the key business assumptions relevant to the plan, including requirements for executive management support, the need for business resource availability, and vendor viability.

12. **Measurement:** Last, we outlined the metrics we would use to measure our plan's success as it unfolded. In our situation, we considered the following metrics and chose one: general staff efficiency improvements, or more specifically, reductions in staff turnover (as was the case in the tax example), attracting new talent, or better staff utilization.

You might also consider including other artifacts and sections as needed. For example, a glossary of terms might be relevant to introduce new concepts. You might like to include a roster of staff members that contributed to your plan. And finally, if the company culture warrants it, include a section that captures management approval of the overall plan.

The Release Plan

While the Capabilities Plan outlines the strategic themes and their execution timeframes, the Release Plan is a detailed blueprint describing the capabilities to be deployed in this release. It includes a detailed narrative as to how the rollout will be managed and which business objectives will be met when completed. Here is an outline of the sections of a comprehensive Release Plan:

1. **Capabilities Overview:** This section summarizes the business technology and capabilities deployed in the release. Use this section to describe the target users impacted by the changes and to document the value derived once implemented.

2. **Release Strategy:** Use this section to outline new capabilities and the teams involved in making this release a success.

    a. **New Capabilities Summary:** Highlight the plan to roll out the new capabilities. Highlight phases if you intend to introduce waves of capabilities during the release.

    a. **Team Responsibilities:** Outline launch roles and responsibilities for the release team (e.g., trainers, project managers, IT resources, business resources, help desk, desktop management, etc.).

    a. **Time Commitment:** For each resource group, outline their anticipated time commitment (as a percentage of someone's time), their responsibilities during the release, and who is leading a specific effort during the release.

    a. **Readiness Checklists:** Use this section to document readiness checklists (e.g., has training been satisfactorily completed, and is the help desk up to speed?).

    a. **Success Metrics:** Highlight the success metrics for this release. This gives management a preview of what to expect when the release is complete.

3. **Pilot Plan:** Use this section to outline plans to pilot new capabilities with limited groups. Sometimes larger, more risky releases are good candidates to pilot with smaller groups. Doing so manages risk and allows you to concentrate on making needed improvements in the rollout prior to a general release to all audiences. Include discrete pilot objectives to document when one phase is complete, and identify when it is ready to move forward with

more users. Highlight the pilot participants and how to test to ensure things are working as planned.

4. **Internal Marketing Plan:** Use this section to develop an overall communication plan. Target all relevant audiences from executive management to the help desk. Lay out a schedule of communication by audience and by communication purpose.

5. **Recovery Plan:** Outline a plan to revert to the old way of doing things in the event the release hits a major speed bump. Document the path of old systems and processes. Include a communication plan and the priority order of communications in the event the rollout needs to stop and back things out. Use this section to identify the triggers that might require backing out (e.g., defect rates or percent of staff impacted). Also, document the processes necessary to address issues and get the release back on track.

6. **Training Plan:** Document the training approach. Describe how training will be accomplished (e.g., online, classroom style, etc.). Identify class availability, trainers, and a list of training materials that will be available for all relevant audiences.

7. **Change Management Plan:** Outline system implementation windows and constraints related to other systems. Outline how to coordinate these changes in concert with any other technology changes planned during the release.

8. **Leadership Change Management:** List the expectations of leaders and individual contributors to the release effort. Describe who is accountable for leading the changes needed in the business unit, in IT, and in the executive team. Create a forum for people to both highlight successes and address issues relating to the release.

9. **Financials:** Include a summary of the financial requirements of the plan. Include relevant staffing, hardware, software,

maintenance costs, hosting fees, and a summary of the hard-dollar benefits related to the release.

The Capabilities Roadmap Tool

A Capabilities Roadmap is a useful tool that offers a high-level snapshot of the overall Capabilities Plan. Use the Capabilities Roadmap to highlight the themes for each collection of releases detailed in the plan. Here is a sample Capabilities Roadmap featuring four overarching theme areas and a proposal for how they should be deployed at this company:

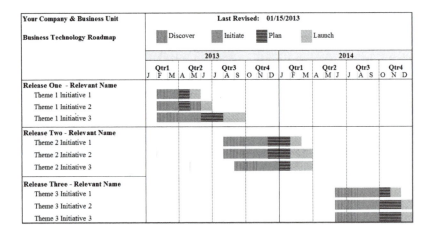

Capability Roadmaps are a quick way to visually show executives the plan's priorities. Add verbal commentary to explain the benefits of each of the plan's release phases. Use these roadmaps to get business leaders engaged in the process and to illustrate what is happening with business units.

Summary: Key IT Business Partnership Tools

Capability Plans, Release Plans, and Capability Roadmaps all connect IT to business goals and objectives and help business unit leaders see the value of leveraging IT to achieve their goals. Use these tools judiciously, and remember to tailor them to your company's culture and style.

Chapter Eleven

Building a Business Case

Once the business unit strategy and Release Plans are complete, the next step is to build a persuasive Business Case to get the investment funded. The Business Case is one of the most compelling ways to highlight the business value that strategic plans deliver; nothing tells the whole story more succinctly. The following chapter details two tools. The first is a Business Case narrative document that outlines the reasons and benefits of the investment. The second tool is a Financial Model that captures the start-up costs, ongoing costs, and benefits for a suite of proposed investments.

The Written Business Case

Think of the written Business Case as a layperson's overview of the investment. As you prepare it, assume that the reader has little or no knowledge of the proposed investment. I sometimes ask a family member to read the written summary to see how readable and clear my writing is. It is fair to assume that readers will know the company's business, but don't assume they are familiar with the details of a service offering or of a department's function.

Keep this narrative as short as possible. If it is too long, executives will become frustrated by having to trudge through it, and this puts them in the wrong frame of mind. Avoid using acronyms as well, as these create unanticipated distractions for some reviewers. This is especially true if they aren't familiar with the in-the-trenches lingo your business unit teams use every day.

Use the section summaries below as a guide to building a strong written Business Case narrative.

1. *Executive Summary*

In this section, provide a high-level summary of the Business Case. Keep it short, clear, and action-oriented. Begin by stating the problem or opportunity followed by a brief narrative on how this proposed investment addresses key business problems. Include a high-level financial summary of the investment. Nothing frustrates executives more than holding off on the financials until the very end of the Business Case. If the high-level finances are not included up front, executives will distract themselves flipping through pages looking for the numbers. Make it easy for them and put a short financial outline right here in the executive summary:

Financial Highlights	Low Estimate	High Estimate
Total Investment Budget	$	$
Capital Expenditure	$	$
ROI (Return on Investment)	%	%
Project Break-even	*Months*	*Months*
NPV (Net Present Value)	$	$

2. *Investment Overview*

This section allows for more details surrounding the investment. Keep each subsection to a paragraph or two. There is no need to rewrite the strategic plan.

2.1 *Problem or Opportunity Statement*

Briefly describe the problem to be solved or opportunity available to the organization.

2.2 Expected Benefits

Enumerate the potential benefits of the investment. A bulleted list is sufficient. This list might include retaining customers, increasing revenue, entering a new market, or reducing operating costs.

2.3 Known Issues, Constraints, and Assumptions

Describe any known issues or constraints associated with the investment. Is this investment dependent on another larger initiative within the organization? Does it require unique new skills or expertise currently not available in the firm? Is there an urgent competitive gap that needs filling?

3. Financial Analysis

Outline the major components of the Financial Model. For smaller-scale projects, this section might be all the financial analysis needed. If so, skip preparing a more detailed spreadsheet. Include information on the following components of the Financial Model:

3.1 Investment Benefits Summary

Highlight the benefits and costs of the investment, and disclose the key performance metrics. Make sure to work with the finance team to get the right metrics into the model. They might also provide guidance on the investment's timeline. The sample below shows three years, but your finance team might suggest a five-year view. There is more about the specific metrics later in this chapter.

Income Statement			
Benefits Summary	Year 1	Year 2	Year 3
Incremental Revenue	$	$	$
Cost Savings	$	$	$
Total Benefits	**$**	**$**	**$**
Start-up/Development Costs			
Total Start-up Costs	$	$	$
Total Operating Expenses	$	$	$
Total Expenses	**$**	**$**	**$**
Key Financial Metrics			
ROI (Return on Investment)			$
NPV (Net Present Value)			$

3.2 Start-up/Development Costs

Summarize the costs of the new investment. Include the purchase of software, servers, temporary staff/consultants, and network gear. This section includes any costs required to establish the capabilities outlined in the investment.

Start-up/Development Cost Summary		
Start-up Costs	Low Estimate	High Estimate
Hardware & Equipment Purchase	$	$
Software License Acquisition	$	$
Other One-Time costs	$	$
Consulting Fees	$	$
Total Development Costs	$	$

3.3 Ongoing/Operating Expenses

Outline the ongoing costs that will reoccur over the investment period. Examples include hardware and software maintenance costs, annual hosting fees, and costs relating to new staff additions driven by the investment.

Operating Expenses		
Operating Expense Summary	Low Estimate	High Estimate
Hardware Support and Maintenance	$	$
Software Support and Maintenance	$	$
Operating Personnel	$	$
Cloud Services / Hosting Fees	$	$
Total Operating Expenses	$	$

3.4 Selling, General, and Administrative Expenses (SG&A)

In this section, summarize expenses relating to training or marketing costs (if this is a new product). Other examples might include applicable taxes or product costs. Be aware that there might not be any incremental SG&A costs for the investment. Work with the finance team to determine the SG&A that is appropriate.

Sales, General, and Administrative Costs		
SG&A	Low Estimate	High Estimate
Sales Promotion and Marketing	$	$
Taxes	$	$
Training Costs	$	$
Total Administrative Expenses	$	$

3.5 Capitalization of Expenses

Determine whether the costs relating to the investment are to be capitalized. Work with the finance team to determine the components and timeframe over which the expenses should be depreciated or amortized. When preparing a full financial statement, show the depreciation and amortization costs spread over the investment time period.

4. Strategic Alignment

Describe how this project aligns with the business unit or company's strategic imperatives. Include a summary of any strategic considerations, along with the impact on earnings, competition, or other possible alternatives.

5. Legal or Compliance Considerations

Describe any legal or regulatory issues that come into play regarding this investment. Highlight the steps and actions required to ensure compliance with existing laws and policies.

6. Risks

In this section, identify the significant risks related to the investment. Once the investment is approved, the Project Management Office will track and manage project-based risks, so don't include them here. Rather, include only those risks that you feel your executive management team should be aware of when reviewing this Business Case. This is a subjective exercise. Consider both the probability of the risk occurring and the severity of the impact (to the schedule, budget, or both) should the risk occur. All projects have risks, but not all projects have risks worth mentioning here. If you decide to include risks in this section, be sure to list them individually. Use specifics and explain how you intend to manage and overcome these risks once the project is underway.

7. *Appendix*

This is an optional section for any artifacts that might help executives better understand the scope and magnitude of the opportunity. Here are some examples:

→ **High-Level Project Milestones:** List any key deliverable milestones. Be sure to highlight that these milestones could change once the PMO puts a more formal plan together.

→ **Financial Details:** If warranted, include more details on vendor costs, hardware costs, and timing of resource additions.

→ **Business Case Team:** Include an overview of the key contributors that developed the Business Case.

→ **Key Vendors:** Include a short summary of the key vendor solutions proposed in the investment.

The Financial Model

The Financial Model is where the rubber meets the road. All of the Business Case financial assumptions will be there for the world to see. Depending on the scope of the request, the Financial Model may be complex and voluminous. I often start with the Financial Model before I create the Business Case narrative. For me, it is helpful to see the full depth and dimension of a particular investment in numbers prior to writing about it.

It is crucial to work with the finance team on this portion of the Business Case. Their blessing on the model is critical to getting over the first approval hurdle. Even if the finance team is not invited to the formal investment approval meeting, one or more executives will likely ask if your model was reviewed by finance. This is one of many good reasons to involve them. Not only are they experts on the financial levers to pull when crafting the finance plan, they are also experts at understanding the company's key financial metrics and how to apply and relate them to the management team's expectations. As an IT Business Partner, familiarize yourself with the financial levers that are available. Understanding them well is part of what will help you sound and act like a true business partner rather than just an IT staff member.

Companies use standard financial terms differently. IT Business Partners should work with the finance team on the specifics of how they use and communicate financial levers and metrics. There are numerous resources on the Internet to help you easily find examples and definitions of common financial terms. The US Small Business Administration (*www.sba.gov*) has a great set of resources that are easy to understand and put to use. Here are definitions for a few of the key metrics and terms in the model:

→ **Capitalization:** This is an accounting method used to delay the recognition of expenses over a period of time. For example, if a company spreads the costs of licensed software over five years, the cost model will reflect one-fifth of the total cost of software each year over a five-year period. Capitalized assets are typically non-tangible (non-physical) assets.

→ **Depreciation:** Like capitalization, depreciation is an accounting method that spreads the cost of a (tangible) asset over time. For example, a computer server might be depreciated over a three-year period. In this case, the server's purchase cost would be reflected in the Business Case as one-third of the total cost of the server for the first three years of the Financial Model.

A note about these techniques:

For depreciation and amortization, companies still need cash to pay for these assets. The benefit of these accounting methods is that a company's profit statement doesn't reflect the full cost of software and hardware all at once. In other words, the company's profit statement only reflects the current period's depreciated or amortized costs of these types of assets.

→ **ROI:** Return on investment is a performance metric used to measure the efficiency of an investment. ROI is almost always expressed as a percentage. Here is the basic formula used to calculate ROI:

$$\frac{\textit{Investment Profit - Investment Cost}}{\textit{Investment Cost}}$$

→ **NPV:** Net present value compares the value of a dollar today versus the value of that dollar in the future. This formula is a bit more complex, so check with the finance team for guidance. NPV is a measurement of all future cash flow (revenues minus costs) that will be derived from an investment, minus the cost of the investment. If the result of the calculation is positive, then the investment makes sense to pursue. Conversely, if the calculation is negative, the investment might not be worth pursuing. Here is a simple example of how NPV works:

If you have $100 to invest and you plan on a 10 percent return, your total position will be $110 at the end of a year. The present value of $110 at 10 percent is $100. The NPV formula takes the original investment of $100 and subtracts it from the present value of $100, yielding a net present value of zero. A net present value that is zero (or greater) means that the investment is a good one.

→ **IRR:** Internal rate of return is the average annual return earned over the life of an investment. It can be calculated in any number of ways, so ask the finance team for guidance. For our purposes here, IRR is used to calculate the discount rate that reduces the net present value to zero. If the IRR is higher than the desired rate of return on investment, then the project is a desirable one.

→ **Profit Margin:** This ratio results from dividing net profit by revenues. This is a useful metric when the investment includes incremental revenue. It isn't as relevant when the investment includes only soft (non-dollar) benefits.

→ **Cash Flow:** This term simply means the movement of cash in or out of the company. When depreciating or amortizing investments, cash flow reflects that actual cash outlay for a server or software license.

→ **Income Statement:** This reflects revenue over a period of time. It also details the costs and expenses associated with earning that revenue.

→ **Profit Statement:** This reflects the revenues, costs, and expenses for a given period. It only shows that period's amortized and depreciated asset costs.

I have used essentially the same Financial Model tool for many years, taking it from company to company and sharing it with colleagues and friends in business. This model is a great starting point in the event your company does not already have a Financial Model in place. What follows are views of the profit statement, cash flow statement, benefits summary, start-up/development costs, and annual operating costs contained in the model.

PROFIT STATEMENT

This is a one-page summary of all of the benefits and costs related to the investment. Tailor the specific line items on the profit statement to your needs. For example, if I knew that my management team would delve more deeply into the benefits of the investment, I might decide to show more rows of benefit details and perhaps summarize more of the operating costs. What you disclose depends on your company's style and culture. In this example, the investment returns a healthy 38.4 percent pre-tax profit margin over the five-year period.

Profit and Loss Statement						
	Year 1	Year 2	Year 3	Year 4	Year 5	TOTALS
PROJECTED REVENUE	$ 762,500	$ 762,500	$ 762,500	$ 762,500	$ 762,500	$ 3,812,500
START-UP COSTS						
Licensed Software	(20,000)	(20,000)	(20,000)	(20,000)	(20,000) $	(100,000)
Client Access License	(35,200)	(35,200)	(35,200)	(35,200)	(35,200)	(176,000)
Consulting	(27,000)	(27,000)	(27,000)	(27,000)	(27,000)	(135,000)
Other Start-up Costs	(5,000)	(5,000)	(5,000)	(5,000)	(5,000)	(411,000)
Total	(87,200)	(87,200)	(87,200)	(87,200)	(87,200)	(436,000)
ANNUAL OPERATING COSTS						
Annual Maintenance Fees	15,200	15,200	15,200	15,200	15,200	76,000
Annual Staffing Expense	(413,250)	(425,648)	(438,417)	(451,569)	(465,117)	(2,194,000)
Other Annual Support Expense	(58,000)	(59,740)	(61,532)	(63,378)	(65,280)	(307,930)
Other Expenses	(1,000)	(1,000)	(1,000)	(1,000)	(1,000)	(5,000)
Total	(457,050)	(471,188)	(485,749)	(500,748)	(516,196)	(2,430,930)
COST OF FUNDS	-	-	-	-	-	-
PROFIT/(LOSS) BEFORE TAX	218,250	204,113	189,551	174,552	159,104	945,570
TAX (LIABILITY)/BENEFIT	(82,935)	(77,563)	(72,029)	(66,330)	(60,460)	(359,317)
NET PROFIT AFTER TAX	$ 135,315	$ 126,550	$ 117,522	$ 108,222	$ 98,644	$ 586,253
Pre-Tax Profit Margin %	28.6%	26.8%	24.9%	22.9%	20.9%	24.8%

CASH FLOW STATEMENT

This view shows the cash outlays relating to software purchases, other licensing costs, consulting costs, and more. It also highlights the annual operating costs and revenue, along with key metrics that rely on cash flow (NPV and IRR specifically). Tailor this page as necessary, showing more or less detail on the annual operating costs and benefits line as needed.

Cash Flow

	Initial	Year 1	Year 2	Year 3	Year 4	Year 5	TOTALS
START-UP COSTS							
Licensed Software	$ 100,000						$ 100,000
Client Access License	176,000						176,000
Consulting	135,000						135,000
Other Start-up Costs	25,000						25,000
TOTAL START-UP COSTS	436,000						436,000
ANNUAL OPERATING COSTS							
Annual Maintenance Fees		(55,200)	(55,200)	(55,200)	(55,200)	(55,200)	(276,000)
Annual Staffing Expense		(413,250)	(425,648)	(438,417)	(451,569)	(465,117)	(2,194,000)
Other Annual Support Expense		(58,000)	(59,740)	(61,532)	(63,378)	(65,280)	(307,930)
Other Expenses		(1,000)	(1,000)	(1,000)	(1,000)	(1,000)	(5,000)
TOTAL OPERATING COSTS		(527,450)	(541,588)	(556,149)	(571,148)	(586,596)	(2,782,930)
PROJECTED REVENUES/BENEFITS		762,500	762,500	762,500	762,500	762,500	3,812,500
COST OF FUNDS (2.5%)	-	-	-	-	-	-	-
NET CASH FLOW	$ (436,000)	$ 235,050	$ 220,913	$ 206,351	$ 191,352	$ 175,904	$ 593,570

Present Value and Internal Rate of Return

Net Present Value @ 15%	267,974
Internal Rate of Return (%)	40.33%

BENEFITS SUMMARY

Here, the benefits summary reflects increased sales revenues from a new product and shows an anticipated reduction in annual consulting costs. In this example, you would take care to explain the plan to achieve the incremental sales and reduce consulting costs. The benefits summary should be included in the Business Case narrative.

Projected Revenue/Benefits

Benefits Summary			Year 1	Year 2	Year 3	Year 4	Year 5	SUMMARY
Revenue	Avg Price	Units						
Increased Sales	$75	7500	$ 562,500	$ 562,500	$ 562,500	$ 562,500	$ 562,500	2,812,500
			$ -	$ -	$ -	$ -	$ -	-
			$ -	$ -	$ -	$ -	$ -	-
			$ -	$ -	$ -	$ -	$ -	-
Total Revenue			$ 562,500	$ 562,500	$ 562,500	$ 562,500	$ 562,500	2,812,500
Cost Savings								
Reduced Consulting			$ 200,000	$ 200,000	$ 200,000	$ 200,000	$ 200,000	1,000,000
			$ -	$ -	$ -	$ -	$ -	-
			$ -	$ -	$ -	$ -	$ -	-
Total Cost Savings			$ 200,000	$ 200,000	$ 200,000	$ 200,000	$ 200,000	1,000,000
Total Benefits			$ 762,500	$ 762,500	$ 762,500	$ 762,500	$ 762,500	3,812,500

START-UP/DEVELOPMENT COSTS

In this example, the costs reflected in the analysis include the cost of purchasing software, seat licenses for a new tool, consulting fees, and training fees. The tool allows a designation for the useful life of the assets. This drives depreciation and amortization calculations so that the costs for the assets are spread appropriately across the investment. In this case, all of the assets are on a five-year depreciation and amortization schedule. The finance team can determine the number of years over which to spread these types of costs. Most likely they have a policy relating to depreciation and amortization and are audited annually by outside auditors, so it is best to follow their standard practices.

Start-up Costs

Licensed Software	Cost			Total		Capitalize	Years
Package 1	$	100,000		$	100,000		
Package 2	$	-		$	-		
Package 3	$	-		$	-		
				$	100,000	Y	5

Client Access License	Cost Per Seat	Seats		Total		Capitalize	Years
Tier One Seats	$	1,000	40	$	40,000		
Tier Two Seats	$	800	20	$	16,000		
Tier Three Seats	$	400	300	$	120,000		
			360	$	176,000	Y	5

Consulting	Hours	Rate		Total		Capitalize	Years
Project Manager	500	$ 100	$	50,000			
Developer	300	$ 100	$	30,000			
Developer	300	$ 100	$	30,000			
BA	250	$ 100	$	25,000			
			$	135,000		Y	5

Other Start-up Costs			Total		Capitalize	Years
Training			$	5,000		
Installation Costs			$	20,000		
			$	25,000	Y	5

Total Start-up Costs			436,000	

ANNUAL OPERATING COSTS

This section details all of the critical annual operating costs for the investment. The example below includes annual maintenance fees and incremental staffing costs. There is an assumption built into this example to show that staffing costs are expected to increase at a rate of 3 percent annually. Of course, the model will need to reflect the cost components relevant to each specific investment. Be cautious about how to reflect ongoing costs in the Financial Model. Some companies include the cost of internal resources. IT Business Partners should discuss this with their finance team.

Annual Operating Expenses							
	%	Year 1	Year 2	Year 3	Year 4	Year 5	SUMMARY
Annual Maintenance Fees							
Licensed Software	20%	$ 20,000	$ 20,000	$ 20,000	$ 20,000	$ 20,000	$ 100,000
Client Access License	20%	$ 35,200	$ 35,200	$ 35,200	$ 35,200	$ 35,200	$ 176,000
		$ (55,200)	$ (55,200)	$ (55,200)	$ (55,200)	$ (55,200)	$ (276,000)
	Annual						
Annual Staffing Expense	Growth %	Salary	Salary	Salary	Salary	Salary	Total
Project Manager	3%	$ 80,000	82,400	84,872	87,418	90,041	424,731
Business Analyst	3%	$ 75,000	77,250	79,568	81,955	84,413	398,185
Developer	3%	$ 75,000	77,250	79,568	81,955	84,413	398,185
User Experience	3%	$ 55,000	56,650	58,350	60,100	61,903	292,002
Total Hours		$ 285,000	293,550	302,357	311,427	320,770	1,513,104
Benefits Rate		45%	45%	45%	45%	45%	NA
Total Staffing Costs		$ (413,250)	(425,648)	$ (438,417)	$ (451,569)	$ (465,117)	$ (2,194,000)
	Annual						
Other Annual Support Expense	Growth %	Salary	Salary	Salary	Salary	Salary	Total
Help Desk	3%	$ 40,000	41,200	42,436	43,709	45,020	212,365
		40,000	41,200	42,436	43,709	45,020	212,365
Benefits Rate		45%	45%	45%	45%	45%	NA
Total Support Costs		$ (58,000)	$ (59,740)	$ (61,532)	$ (63,378)	$ (65,280)	$ (307,930)

Leveraging the Finance Team

A Business Case's strongest supporter is the finance team, and their contributions to your financial analysis are critical. Getting the finance department's approval first eliminates potential questions that might arise later if Financial Models are not thoroughly vetted or pre-approved. If they have a standard Financial Model tool, consider using it. It is easier to conform to an existing standard than to forge a new one on your own. If ideas presented here can be incorporated into the company's existing financial standard, be sure to work with the finance department to make that happen. Decision makers are intimately acquainted with their existing format, making it easier for them to understand the financial parameters detailed in the model. In general, using existing finance-team resources to build the Financial Model component of a Business Case ensures that the process will go smoothly in the next phase.

Pre-selling: An Effective Way to Garner Support and Overcome Obstacles

A lot is riding on getting the strategy and funding approved. Prior to seeking formal approval for any strategy or funding proposal, take the package on the road. Meet with key decision makers and stakeholders one-on-one to review the plan with them. Doing so gives them an opportunity to weigh in on the ideas in a safe setting. They can ask questions they might not be willing to ask in a more public forum. When they do, an opportunity occurs to incorporate their feedback and make adjustments prior to seeking more formal approval. This exercise builds trust, makes the presentation stronger, and identifies beforehand those individuals who might not be supportive of the case. If you come across someone who is dead set against approval, enlist business unit leaders to head off a potential issue down the road.

I remember employing these tactics for over 18 months to get a large-scale $20M project approved. It took numerous conversations and lots of tweaking before the leadership team was ready to move forward. The ideas presented in our plan were solidly backed by field research, Financial Models, written Business Cases, and strong links to competitors and customers. Still, our company hadn't embarked on a project of this size and scale in decades. After many rounds of adjusting the messaging and Business Case, I finally felt ready to present it to the board of directors. I remember the day well. I had butterflies, and the adrenaline was pumping.

Our management team was invited to board meetings on a regular basis and we knew the board members well. Given our company culture, though, I didn't meet with any of them (except my boss and his boss) prior to the meeting. On the big day I gave my presentation and the board grilled me with questions. Thanks to the many pre-approval, one-on-one meetings I had with stakeholders, many of them chimed in to help me field the board's questions, and even voiced their own approval. Because I knew I already had the support of the management team, I didn't feel like I was up there alone, and this increased my confidence as I addressed the board.

I remember the intense excitement at getting their formal approval, but then just as quickly I experienced a moment of panic: "Oh, wow. Now we really have to get this done!" I had worked so long to get to this point and now suddenly all the talking was over. It was time to launch the project, secure some early wins, and then keep the momentum building.

In hindsight, asking the board for approval at that meeting was anticlimactic. The funding was ultimately approved because we took a collaborative approach and completed so much rigorous legwork first. The invaluable field research, early meetings with stakeholders, finance approvals on the numbers, and one-on-one previews with executive management were all prerequisite to approval. Building a truly comprehensive Business Case is tedious work, but it remains the best way to ensure the selection and funding of the types of powerful initiatives that drive business results.

In general, all investments need a Business Case. Larger-scale financial investments demand more rigor and analysis. Smaller-scale projects may only require an abbreviated summary. Tailor the tools outlined in this chapter to fit the culture of your company and the size and scope of the investment request.

Summary: *The Rubber Meets the Road*

Financial Models tend to get more complicated the larger the investment is and the greater the number of vendor solutions to be incorporated. IT Business Partners need time to think through the design of each Financial Model. Remember that there really are only a few key areas to cover:

→ One-time start-up costs

→ Ongoing costs

→ Benefits

Getting these components roughed out gives IT Business Partners all the levers they need to create a solid Financial Model. Once these components are nailed down, IT Business Partners need to think through the details they would like to share on the summary pages, especially the profit and cash flow pages. This is where the executive team will begin their review. Having a strong finance partner to assist with the Financial Model component of the Business Case is fundamental to its success.

There is nothing glamorous about building Business Cases, but they do reveal the potential of investments more succinctly and clearly than any other IT Business Partner tool. Business Cases establish business acumen and credibility with the executive management team. IT Business Partners should work closely with the finance team to make sure the company's metrics and financial standards are baked into the process.

Chapter Twelve

Understanding How Your Company Competes

A number of years ago, while I was working in the securities industry, I heard a well-known economist speak about companies and their successes and failures. He said something that I have never forgotten: "The market is brutally efficient: it weeds out bad ideas and poor leaders and it never fails to do so—it is only just a matter of time." Being a good IT Business Partner means being a good leader, and to be a good leader, you need to have an intimate and nuanced knowledge of how your company competes. Here are some suggestions to help peel back the layers.

How Does Your Company Make Money?

If asked how their company makes money, many people would glibly answer, "All a company has to do is take in more money than it spends." It sounds simple, but as we all know, there is more than that to the story. For IT Business Partners, that simple answer just isn't enough, and it probably shouldn't be for any truly engaged employee. Start by asking leaders in your firm how your company makes money. IT Business Partners may feel embarrassed if they don't already know, but the open-ended nature of the question can lead to some interesting conversations and a greater appreciation of them as an employee.

GET TO KNOW YOUR CUSTOMERS

To get a real understanding of how a company makes money, start by getting to know its customers. Try and learn as much as possible about their connection to the company. Why did they select the company? Why do they stick with it? If a customer decides to move to a competitor, find out why. Research how the company wins or loses customers to gain insight into what is working and what needs to improve. Look into finding out the same about the company's competitors.

ASK NEWLY HIRED EMPLOYEES

A great way to learn about competitors might come from right inside the company itself. If there are new employees that recently joined the firm from a competitor, set up some time to learn what they liked at that firm and what they didn't. Try to uncover what their customers liked and didn't like about their products or services. Get the new employee's perspective on their impressions of your company while they are still fresh. Once they are with the company for even a short period of time, those perceptions will likely be forgotten.

LEVERAGE SOCIAL MEDIA AND THE WEB

Competitor information is easier to gather now than ever in the past. Social media, company websites, and the richness of content on the Internet make it easier to research former customers and competitors. I had a product manager that worked for me a number of years ago who began pioneering these skills when company websites began to proliferate across the Internet. He would routinely scan competitor career sites. When we saw that these firms were hiring developers, we guessed that they were working on a major new release of a competitive software product. It turned out we were always right.

It didn't necessarily change our plans, but it did give us a little time to get our own product offering in order.

One unique aspect of social media is that anyone can listen in on customer conversations taking place at just about any company on the planet. It is reasonable to assume that competitors are also listening to your customers. To listen in and stay current, sign up for email alerts from company websites. Join their Facebook pages. Follow them on Twitter and on LinkedIn. LinkedIn has become a great place to see what the competitors' employees are up to. To learn about the consumer goods market, routinely check out product reviews on Amazon and eBay. These are all valuable resources that will help you stay up-to-date on what customers think of your company's products and the competitors' too.

THE ERA OF THE CUSTOMER

We have entered an unprecedented era in which customers drive corporate agendas more than they ever have in the past. Using a combination of social media, mobile devices, cloud computing, and the proliferation of online information, customers now define their own consumer experiences with companies. The technology research firm Gartner refers to this phenomenon as the "Nexus of Forces." While the implications aren't fully understood, businesses have to become even more adaptable than ever before by making products and services available in the manner that suits customers, who expect seamless and consistent shopping experiences whether they are shopping in a store, online, or with a smartphone. In fact, more and more customers are completely redefining the fundamental notion of what it means to "shop" and "buy." For IT Business Partners, connecting with customers and conducting field research has never been more important in terms of understanding the constantly shifting requirements of today's consumer.

In this era of the customer, it is crucial to conduct field research to see how customers interact with your organization. In the past, IT could pick a platform and standardize go-to-market solutions. In a world dominated by the Nexus of Forces, that will be difficult, if not impossible. For example, it is anyone's guess as to which manufacturer will win the day on mobile devices. In fact, even the very notion of what it means to "win the day on mobile devices" has changed. In today's world, companies are zooming toward their zenith and then just as quickly being replaced by another rising star in a kind of developmental leapfrog.

The old definition of market domination included some component of time—how long a company held on to the top market position. Nowadays, the duration of any one product line or even an entire company can be much shorter and still be a financial success. IT organizations will just have to get used to the idea that investing in mobile computing will be a roller-coaster ride and that code bases will have to be rewritten or even abandoned as market forces and consumers choose the winners.

It is an exciting time, like no other we have lived through thus far. IT Business Partners must focus on how to effectively embrace the cloud, deliver solutions on any device, and mine customer and market insights through intelligent analytics, all while keeping company and consumer assets safe and secure.

There is no denying that the Nexus of Forces will make some processes and architectures obsolete. IT Business Partners will have to filter business opportunities, vendor partners, and future business technology investments through the lens of this nexus. They will need to look for cross-dependencies between cloud, mobile, social, and information dimensions.

Successful IT Business Partners must have a fundamental understanding of what makes their company work. Getting familiar with customers both in terms of why they select a company or why they don't shapes strategic initiatives. Customers determine where to take the business unit and ultimately, the company. Hyper-adaptability will become the new normal for IT organizations and companies as a whole. The challenge as an IT Business Partner is to stay informed and engaged and to be the business unit's eyes and ears.

What Does Your Company Value?

When I was first introduced to the concept of product management in the mid-1990s, Michael Treacy and Fred Wiersema had just written the book *The Discipline of Market Leaders*. It made its way through our organization and caused quite a stir. The premise of the book was simple. The authors suggested that there are three value disciplines that companies should adapt to be successful. The three disciplines are product leadership, customer intimacy, and operational excellence. They suggested that companies have to be great at just one of the disciplines and good enough at the other two. They made the point that it is hard for companies to achieve greatness in all three dimensions because of inherent conflicts between them. For example, creating the best product is not always operationally efficient. Understanding which of the three disciplines drives your company will provide guidance when weighing the merits of conflicting investments.

Business leaders in our company became annoyed with the premise of the book. They were irritated that so many emerging leaders within the company were asking questions about the three disciplines as they applied to us and our company. I honestly think that some of that frustration came from not knowing how to answer the question. Regardless, the book and its teachings made an impact. As an emerging product manager in the software industry, I was inspired to think about the investments we were making in our products and how they aligned with our company's strengths. Our firm was known for its great software products. We took great pride in delivering the best capabilities in the market. Some of our executives cited customer intimacy as our greatest strength. I think it was hard for them to not think of us that way, especially when talking to customers, shareholders, or the board of directors. What leader wants to admit that customer intimacy is not a core strength of its company?

Some of our leadership team drew battle lines and took either the product leader or the customer intimacy side of the line. It was a silly game we were playing internally. Our position of product leadership didn't mean we had permission from the market to be horrible at customer service, and we weren't, for that matter. Thankfully, things did settle down after a period of time and we resumed our practice of being a great product company.

What the authors' insights taught us is that the value proposition for each discipline is different. Companies that focus on operational excellence concentrate on delivering the best total value, while customer-intimate companies focus on providing the best total solution; companies that are product leaders concentrate on producing the best possible products. When investment decisions surfaced, this framework oriented our thinking around the value proposition that best suited our company's mission, and it put investment dollars to work on the right initiatives. Understanding the company's value proposition helps IT Business Partners engage with business leaders, and it provides needed guardrails when sorting out which investments to pursue.

Rising Customer Expectations

Market forces have raised the bar on all three disciplines. Still, focusing on one of the three does make sense. One such market force, omni-channel commerce, is having a profound impact on retailers.

The premise of omni-channel is simple: make the consumer-shopping experience a great one and appropriately consistent at all distribution points. This means delivering on a company's brand promise faithfully whether customers are buying in brick-and-mortar stores, shopping online, on smartphones, or in a fleet of mobile stores. Many consumer goods manufacturers and retailers have embarked on omni-channel commerce initiatives, as it is the next logical step in the holy grail of retailing.

Retailers are competing in a world where the bar is being continually raised by companies like Amazon, Best Buy, eBay, and Zappos. For example, same-day shipping and no-cost returns shape consumer-buying expectations. Shipping within 48 hours is not an option anymore: to remain competitive, retailers must get products out the door within 24 hours to keep customers happy. You might argue that the bar for "good enough" has been raised and this is now every supply chain team's challenge. All eyes will be on them to work miracles. In the end, successful retailers will need an infusion of capital improvements to enable consistent shipping within 24 hours, something retailers didn't have to do before omni-channel commerce and the advent of the Nexus of Forces.

Summary: Market Insight Matters

Understanding your company and its competitors, knowing what customers think of your products or services versus others, and recognizing the ramifications of social media sites will significantly impact your performance as an IT Business Partner. Incorporating information about competitors and their products and services, and knowing what customers say about your company, all contribute to increasing the IT Business Partner's credibility as a trusted advisor. Finally, awareness of the key disciplines that drive the company will help you make better investment decisions.

Chapter Thirteen

Managing Inside Your Company

IT Business Partners have a unique opportunity to work across the entire company. They belong to more than one team. In fact, they play an important role on many teams. They must influence people within the IT organization and in the business units they serve, and they have to convince executive management to make investments that they might not want to endorse at first glance. Earning a reputation as a can-do resource paves the way for their success.

This chapter focuses on the skills needed to network internally to earn the trust and confidence of the teams you serve. To be clear, this chapter isn't about IT Business Partners working their own agenda or "managing up" in the conventional sense. Rather, it is about promoting the IT organization and the business units' priorities, goals, and accomplishments.

Embrace Office Politics

Office politics are a part of life in companies, and being cognizant of them is necessary to survive and do well. The reality is there just aren't many companies, private or public, large or small, free of office politics. An esteemed colleague of mine used to say that the only way to avoid office politics is to retire. Before taking that dramatic step, try thinking about office politics differently. Embrace them as an opportunity to become more effective in accomplishing goals in the workplace. Let's start with a new definition of managing up; share it with IT Business Partners and the entire IT organization.

> *Managing Up:* When meeting with your boss's boss or your boss's peers, the primary objective must be to promote your boss, your team, and/or your peers. You should never go over your boss's head to curry favor with your own people, to work your personal career agenda, or to play politics at your boss's expense. In other words, only go over your boss's head to let his or her superiors know how great they are and how great their team is. If you can't consistently find some aspect of their performance to tout positively, then it might be time to switch jobs or bosses.

This definition was inspired by the author August Turak, who writes about service and selflessness in a *Forbes* magazine article, "The 11 Leaderships Secrets You Never Heard About." He was a former colleague of the iconic author Jim Collins, and his notion of loyalty is compelling. Frankly, this definition is a great one for all leaders. Share it with business unit leadership teams and let them know that you are making every attempt to live by this definition each time you meet with anyone around the firm. It is easy to have sidebar conversations when you are frustrated about a decision your boss or business unit leaders have or haven't made. But remember to keep conversations constructive, thereby developing a positive perception.

IT Business Partners Must Be Visible

It was John Donne, a sixteenth-century English poet, who wrote, "No man is an island." This oft quoted line is relevant for IT Business Partners too. People around the company have a natural curiosity about what is happening. Some people proactively seek out information, while others wait for it to come to them. IT Business Partners will find it helpful to develop a communication game plan that enables employees to listen in on what is happening in their world. Employees want to hear about the investments that IT Business Partners are working on as well as the investments whose merits are in the process of being debated, and they want to get insight into what directions IT might take further down the road.

COMMUNICATE PROACTIVELY

There are a number of ways to accomplish proactive communication with an organization, and no one method works best. When multiple ways to share the current news of IT Business Partner efforts are available, people can choose the option that best suits them. Regardless of the approach, don't get discouraged with the people who will inevitably still say they don't know what is happening and that they wish they knew more. In fact, some studies show that for these people, the more communication there is, the more they say they don't hear anything. Concentrate on reaching the people who genuinely want to stay informed, and do not concern yourself with the others.

SEVEN WAYS TO DISSEMINATE IT PROJECT INFORMATION

1. Hold Lunch-and-Learn Sessions

Lunch-and-learn sessions have long been a staple of learning organizations. Lunch is a great time to conduct information update sessions. The informal settings generate a safe place to ask questions. In larger, more public settings, people are more likely to clam up during Q&As. The lunch-and-learn sessions should be intimate and informal. Budget allowing, bring in dessert and encourage people to linger informally and even one-on-one. Regardless of the format, people are more likely to gather if they can eat. If the company has a wellness program, include healthy choices in addition to the standard office gathering fare. Partnering with the HR team on that front can win support internally.

2. *Create an Internal Blog*

   If the company has an Intranet (and if it doesn't, consider starting one), set up a blog to share ideas and engage employees at the same time. Not everyone will follow the blog, but this approach appeals to those who are genuinely interested in engaging. Blogging is an easy but visible way to have a public conversation with anyone in the company willing to jump in and get involved.

3. *Attend Business Unit Team Meetings*

   Many business unit teams conduct recurring all-hands meetings. Work with meeting organizers to get on the agenda. Tailor the message to this audience. For example, a finance team might be more interested in the underlying Financial Model for a recent investment. Consider previewing the investment budget with them by providing a financial update. HR might be more interested in new hires and on-boarding, the sales organization in customer training and availability dates, etc.

4. *Send Out Email Blasts*

   For important cross-organization announcements, consider an email blast to an entire department or the whole company. Be aware that this has the potential to make people feel like they are being spammed from inside their own company. Use this option sparingly, for larger, feel-good topics such as funding approvals, launch announcement dates, or successes.

5. *Establish a Site on Your Company Intranet*

For many key programs and projects, using an Intranet site to house relevant information about initiatives works well. Since so many different parts of an organization are involved in large-scale initiatives, creating a spot to share documents and communication is often well received. I have seen PMOs include project status reports, issue-tracking documents, charters, and all manner of project-based documents on sites like this. Using a site that supports alerts gives employees the option to sign up for them as fits their interest level.

6. *Use Quizzes or Surveys on your Intranet*

Consider using Intranet surveys or quizzes. Make them fun by including simple, inexpensive giveaways that motivate people to participate. I worked for a company that would routinely use their Intranet site for scavenger hunts. These were based on finding the correct answer to a business question relating to a project. The prizes don't have to be elaborate or expensive. People like to play a bit and have fun in the office. Winners like to tout their successes, and that can generate positive buzz around the company.

7. *Conduct Mini Conferences*

We have all attended conferences where there is an exhibitors' hall. Consider setting up tables in a common area, like vendors do at trade shows, and hand out relevant facts or brochures about a key investment. This approach creates an informal way to have conversations with employees about programs. People on their way to the cafeteria or break room can stop for five minutes to get a product preview or learn about upcoming training on a given initiative.

The Importance of Face Time

Face time is crucial to establishing and maintaining relationships, no matter what kind you are trying to build. Getting face time with key business unit leaders and project stakeholders is a great way to make emotional connections. Build a list of key stakeholders and make a plan for regular face-to-face interaction. Take time to prepare an agenda of topics to review before each meeting. The more IT Business Partners get to know each stakeholder's hot-button issues, the earlier they can head off any potential problems. IT Business Partners will also be better positioned to seek stakeholder help when things go off the rails, as they sometimes do on large-scale projects.

WHEN RELATIONSHIPS AREN'T NURTURED

I once worked in an organization where we were in the middle of a major systems and business process upgrade. It was the first of its kind in over a decade. One of the stakeholders, though he was not on the executive management team, was a quiet but forceful figure in the company. For storytelling purposes, I will refer to this individual as Gene. Gene was a long-time employee at the firm. He worked in the finance organization for many years, and at one point had been responsible for the IT organization.

I had a so-so working relationship with Gene. I wouldn't say it was bad, but it certainly hadn't been properly nurtured or cared for. My team worked extraordinarily hard to get funding for much-needed improvements in our tools and processes. I made the pitch with our IT Business Partner team and received the funding we asked for.

As it turned out, Gene had been instrumental in establishing the previous platform and business processes we were now looking to upgrade, and he took great pride in this accomplishment. Despite his successes, he was notorious in the company for his direct style, and he had a reputation for intimidating people by talking down to them. He even had T-shirts made with the words "cold heartless bastard" emblazoned on them to promote his style of management. Gene took great joy in flexing his corporate muscles whenever he could.

My tendency was to give him a wide berth and stay out of his way. That turned out to be a big mistake. When our project reached a bumpy point, we needed Gene and his team's help to find our way out of the problem. When I asked him to lend a hand, he verbally agreed that he would, but in actuality he didn't back up his promise with any real or meaningful action. I soon learned that behind the scenes Gene was badmouthing both the project and the IT organization. For example, even though he had initially recommended the vendor we eventually chose, publically he questioned IT's vendor decision and even began spreading his doubts across the organization. The situation grew worse as the project progressed.

In hindsight, if I had proactively engaged Gene and made him the project sponsor at the beginning of the program, things would have turned out differently. Instead, I inadvertently alienated him by not involving him in ways that respected his previous contributions to the organization. Subconsciously I was probably ignoring him; who wants to deal with a self-professed "cold heartless bastard"? I certainly didn't at the time, and so I let our relationship atrophy by avoiding him when, in fact, I should have been taking the opposite approach and scheduling face time with him.

The project went on and was eventually implemented, though with many more bumps than were good for the company, which meant more stress than its employees deserved. The company gave Gene tacit permission to act the way he did by neglecting to stop his behavior along the way. But even within that unhealthy environment there was much more I could have done to positively impact the situation and garner his support. Whether you are in a healthy corporate climate or not, don't surrender your power by skipping face time.

Summary: Cultivate and Nurture Relationships

The concepts presented here might not seem terribly exciting or revolutionary, but consider these ideas within the framework of what powerful IT Business Partnerships make possible. Suddenly, embracing office politics is an opportunity to make headway and realize success. IT Business Partners that leverage these concepts create strong teams that collaborate enthusiastically. There is much to be gained for IT Business Partners when they make it a point to be positive and visible, and when they rely on the tried-and-true practices of good office politics and managing up to accomplish business goals.

Chapter Fourteen

Collaboration and Teams

The previous chapter stressed the importance of building strong relationships, being visible, and making sure IT Business Partners have face time with key stakeholders. This chapter explores collaboration and a few team dynamic techniques that will further improve the chances of IT Business Partnership success. While IT Business Partners may not be directly responsible for teams, understanding what makes them work well provides a significant advantage. In addition, these skills will allow IT Business Partners to spot and overcome the effects of poor team dynamics.

There are many excellent resources available on the subject of teams. My intention here is to provide practical tools to use tomorrow, in the office, right out of the box. In particular, I am a big fan of Patrick Lencioni, author of *The Five Dysfunctions of a Team*, and of Daniel Goleman, author of *Emotional Intelligence*. These thought leaders and their concepts are fundamental in terms of establishing and maintaining good team performance.

A Model for High-Performing Teams

If you haven't read Lencioni's book, I encourage you to do so. The concepts are sound and easy to grasp. However, it takes patience and real commitment to implement them. Recently, as part of a CIO

Mentor coaching engagement, I used these principles while working with a bright, energetic CIO and his team. Their organization was experiencing problems both in and outside of IT, so this CIO asked me to take his group through the fundamentals of successful team dynamics. I shared my experience with Lencioni's team pyramid concept described in *The Five Dysfunctions of a Team*. The name of the book itself can make some people bristle, so as I introduced the model, I was careful to point out that I wasn't labeling their team as dysfunctional. This is the conclusion I knew they would probably jump to, given the lack of trust within the team and with their leadership in general.

UNDERSTANDING THE HISTORY AND
CULTURE OF AN ORGANIZATION

The CIO of this organization and I knew that one training program wouldn't change a legacy of challenges within this firm. Still, hoping for at least some improvement, I conducted interviews with the firm's executives. Privately they volunteered that employees suffered from a long history of micromanagement, a lack of empowerment, and silo thinking. You could feel the tension in the air. These issues permeated the entire organization, not just IT.

Later, as I took the team through the layers of Lencioni's pyramid, we explored how trust, healthy debate, commitment, accountability, and results worked in their organization. The conversation was good, but it was clear that people were not open to being vulnerable or telling the truth. Interestingly, those that had been with the firm for less than a year were the most vocal. They offered authentic observations, though much of what people had to say was non-specific and superficial. We ended the session that day and asked the team to think about what they had learned. We gave them a homework assignment prior to our next scheduled workshop to apply some of what we had covered. We planned a future all-day, in-depth workshop hoping to pull staff members out of their comfort zones and into a mindset where they would feel comfortable sharing honest perspectives regarding life within their company and team.

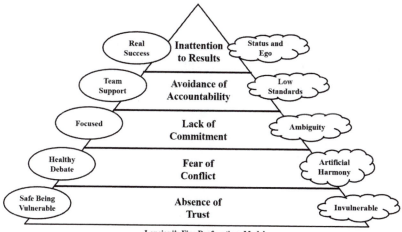

Lencioni's Five Dysfunctions Model

A few days after our initial session, a team member who I'll call George sent a scathing email to the CIO. In it, George demanded to know why I was even there; he felt they could tackle team-building on their own. He railed on the firm's leadership team, saying that this was just another program-of-the-month and a waste of money. He complained that the firm had already tried these things before but nothing had ever changed. He also claimed that I had called their team dysfunctional and that Lencioni's message was antiquated, resembling a trite management concept from the early 1950s.

INVOLVE EMPLOYEES IN THE SOLUTION

George was full of rage, and his email, which he unwisely chose to share with his boss, was little more than a venting session criticizing his leadership team. The CIO of the firm, who I'll call Evan, called me to ask what he should do. His initial idea was to reprimand George and ask for an apology. We thought about it and agreed that instead, it would be much better if he were to ask George to rewrite his note, this time with constructive and thoughtful suggestions.

Evan did just that. He thanked George for taking time to write so many comments and acknowledged that he could see how passionate George was about the issues. He pointed out, however, that in the email's current format, he wasn't able to take action on any of the points and asked for clearer, more positive recommendations. He assured George that he wanted to use his feedback to make things better. George's assignment was to rewrite the note, making sure that only actionable items were offered up.

Surprising Results

George reluctantly took this challenge. A few days later, George asked Evan for a meeting. In that session, George broke down. He told Evan that he had bought Lencioni's book, read it, and realized that he was, as he put it, "the jerk" mentioned in the book. He made a full apology. He told Evan that he'd had a difficult time rewriting the memo and that from that moment on he would be committing himself to becoming a better team member. Evan capitalized on the moment to thank George for being authentic. Evan made it safe for George to speak his mind and ultimately, to expose his vulnerability. In doing so, they formed a stronger bond and began to build the trust team members need to perform at optimum levels.

It was a great story with a positive ending. I certainly didn't expect those results after only one session. Evan and I concurred that breakthroughs like George's are only possible when someone is ready to make a change and they have a supportive environment in which to do so. No matter how much groundwork we lay as managers and IT Business Partners, individuals must decide when they are ready to make a change.

IT Business Partners who can show their own vulnerabilities earn the trust of those they serve. Business units and IT team members recognize IT Business Partner honesty and in turn more readily trust that IT Business Partners are there to help them succeed. With trust established, healthy conflict, commitment, accountability, and real results all become increasingly possible.

Fight or Flight

When people feel threatened physically or even socially, their fight-or-flight reflex tends to kick in, even in traditional office environments. This basic human instinct is so strong you can see it in real time when people are arguing, as they react predominantly with their emotions. I often wish I could hit a pause button and give them time to gain control. I was once in a team-building session with my direct reports when our facilitator introduced us to the amygdala, the brain region that controls the fight-or-flight reflex. We all shared stories, some personal and some from the office, of people losing control and not being able to think clearly.

BRAIN SCIENCE

The amygdala is a powerful organ. It triggers emotions faster than conscious awareness and contains circuits that the brain responds to in the face of what it perceives to be significant emotional events before any other part of the brain has a chance to. The amygdala is there to protect us from harm by interpreting subconscious hints of danger and triggering lightning-fast responses. These instincts serve us well in the wild but not so well in the office. This is what leads to those uncomfortable office exchanges when people aren't thinking clearly and fall victim to each other's emotional outbursts.

Remember the old adage "Count to ten when angry"? Well, there is something to that. Pausing for a moment allows us to consciously move past our emotional state and beyond the instinctive fight-or-flight reflex. It gives us time to rationalize the situation and to consider a more thoughtful, cerebral response to a stressful situation. Thinking back to George's initial email, he was clearly swirling around in his amygdala when he wrote his inflammatory email. We later talked about the fight-or-flight reflex in our in-depth team-building session, and George volunteered his story to the team. When we broke into smaller groups, we asked people to share stories about their fight-or-flight experiences in the office. People enjoyed recounting their stories, and it helped to reinforce the notion that when feeling that urge to fight, all we need to do is pause for a few seconds to allow our brains to catch up and move on to more rational thought.

There is no doubt that IT Business Partners will face emotional episodes. There are frustrated people that have been waiting a lifetime (at least in their minds) for a project request. This leads to what I call "amygdala moments." IT Business Partners are on the front lines of the request process and will encounter frustrated users, especially in the early stages of a new IT Business Partnership program. When this happens, just remember to pause for a bit before formulating a response. Staying calm and rational sends the message that no matter the circumstance, IT Business Partners can be trusted to be composed and approachable. This reinforces the idea that they can be counted on as a true leader.

Self-Assessment

A tool that I use to evaluate my own performance is Daniel Goleman's Emotional Intelligence model. In his groundbreaking research, Goleman asserts that while we are born with a certain intellectual IQ potential, emotional intelligence can be learned. Whatever a person's natural starting point, anyone can make huge improvements in their own EQ simply by becoming more mindful of their behavior.

Dimensions of Emotional Intelligence

	Definition	Hallmarks
Self-Awareness	Knowing one's emotions, strengths, weaknesses, drives, values, and their impact on others	• Self-confidence • Realistic self-assessment • Self-deprecating sense of humor
Self-Regulation	Controlling or redirecting disruptive impulses and moods	• Trustworthiness and integrity • Comfort with ambiguity • Openness to change
Motivation	Relishing achievement for its own sake	• Strong drive to achieve • Optimism, even in the face of failure • Organizational commitment
Empathy	Understanding other people's emotional makeup and considering others' feelings, especially when making decisions	• Expertise in leading change • Cross-cultural sensitivity • Service to clients and customers
Social Skill	Building rapport with others to move them in a desired direction	• Effectiveness in leading change • Persuasiveness • Expertise in building and leading teams

IT Business Partners with high EQ outperform those that have lower EQ or who are just generally not self-aware. People who can't see their own weaknesses or how they are perceived by others are unlikely to excel in the nuanced relationships and collaboration that define the IT Business Partner role. The inevitable outcome is missed opportunity and substandard business results.

COACHING WITH EMOTIONAL INTELLIGENCE

I was once working with an IT Business Partner that had low self-awareness. We worked on this issue for a period of time using real office scenarios as our lesson plans. This individual also had difficulty staying out of his amygdala. He was quick to respond to challenges with emotion and defensiveness. After working together for a period of time, it was clear that though he had made improvements, he just did not seem capable of making the changes required to be a successful IT Business Partner. We both decided that it would be best for him to move on. Sometimes that realization is enough to shake someone out of their funk, though it might still be too late. Once someone earns a reputation for amygdala-type responses, it's hard to change that perception.

It wasn't until after he left the company that this person acknowledged his contributions to the problem. Upon reflection, he could see that his behavior and lack of self-awareness brought unneeded tension and conflict to the team. It turned out that the EQ model was difficult for him to look at objectively. The individual had a hard time being honest about his own abilities. It takes a strong, mature, and confident individual to take honest stock of their performance and to acknowledge their less-than-desirable traits.

I took Goleman's original article on emotional intelligence and turned it into the following self-assessment model. Use the EQ model when there are tense moments during the day as a way to reflect on interactions and contributions to conflict. This process trains the brain to bypass the fight-or-flight instinct and achieve more rational thought earlier the next time a similar situation occurs. With solid EQ, IT Business Partners are more likely to establish trust with their business units. Business leaders will see that IT Business Partners are capable of being a safe haven for discussion even when they disagree with strategy or tactics.

Self-Assessment					
1=Never, 2=Rarely, 3=Sometimes, 4=Frequently, 5=Always	1	2	3	4	5
Self-Awareness					
Emotional Self-Awareness: the ability to read and understand your emotions as well as recognize their impact on work performance, relationships, and the like.					
Accurate Self-Assessment: a realistic evaluation of your strengths and limitations.					
Self-Confidence: a strong and positive sense of self-worth.					
Self-Management					
Self-Control: the ability to keep disruptive emotions and impulses under control.					
Trustworthiness: a consistent display of honesty and integrity.					
Conscientiousness: the ability to manage changing situations and overcome obstacles.					
Achievement Orientation: the drive to meet an internal standard of excellence.					
Initiative: a readiness to seize opportunities.					
Social Awareness					
Empathy: skill in sensing other people's emotions, understanding their perspectives, and taking an active interest in their concerns.					
Organizational Awareness: the ability to read the currents of the organizational life, build decision networks, and navigate politics.					
Service Orientation: the ability to recognize and meet the customer's needs.					
Social Skill					
Visionary Leadership: the ability to take charge and inspire with a compelling vision.					
Influence: the ability to wield a range of persuasive tactics.					

Lessons from the World of Improv

One of the companies I worked for decided to put a bit of fun into our learning-and-development program. We visited the famed Second City Improv Company in Chicago, which has launched the careers of many famous *Saturday Night Live* comedy stars. At the time, our organization was focused on adapting a major company-wide change initiative. We were embarking on a business transformation project unlike any we had tackled in decades. We chose Second City because who understands adaptability and teamwork better than improvisational performance artists?

Admittedly, many of us initially thought this would be more of a fun exercise than anything practically useful. We were wrong! The lessons we learned from their communications program caught on quickly and have stayed with us ever since. Even the most rigid members of our team got on board. What we liked most about the Second City concepts is that they were ready to use right away.

Coincidentally, I was, at the time, a co-chair of a regional CIO executive summit in the Twin Cities. The organizers brought us together to work on the agenda for an upcoming annual event. They too brought in a local improv company, The Brave New Workshop in Minneapolis, to get our creativity flowing. The Brave New Workshop taught our CIO group some of the same communication skills that we had been exposed to at Second City.

The following concepts are tools from the world of improvisational comedy that can make IT Business Partners more effective by creating a collaborative and supportive culture in any company.

IMPROV TOOLS

1. **Use the phrase "Yes, and . . ."** Use this phrase when responding to a comment as a technique to support and encourage open communication. By saying yes first, you acknowledge that you hear the other person's message and understand their point of view. The "and" part of the "yes, and . . ." prompts you to constructively build on their point as a way of sharing your own point of view. It seems like a simple idea and frankly, it is. When this technique is used over a period of time, collaboration and trust between teammates is strengthened in a way that pays dividends down the road.

2. **Love every idea for a little bit.** When every suggestion is given consideration, ideas or angles that you might have otherwise discounted too quickly become visible. Honor and respect the differences people bring to the table and fully explore their creativity by instituting a program that avoids rejecting ideas out of hand, no matter how silly they might initially seem.

3. **Play the scene you are in, not the one you rehearsed.** In other words, drop the script. Be open to playing with new ideas at least briefly, even if they don't meet with conventional wisdom.

4. **Bring a brick, not a cathedral.** Don't try and solve problems all on your own. Let ideas grow by truly leveraging different perspectives one step at a time. By doing so, you are more likely to get buy-in to the end solution.

5. **Use "you could" instead of "you should."** By paying attention to word choice and how emotions influence your message, you are more likely to encourage open and creative thinking.

Summary: Teamwork Equals High Performance

IT Business Partners by definition work with many teams: their business unit, IT, and finance, to name a few. Understanding Lencioni's concept of high-performing teams, becoming aware of the fight-or-flight instinct, working to improve EQ, and taking lessons from the world of improv all contribute to better IT Business Partner performance. Some people try to minimize the skills described in this chapter by defining them as soft skills. Those who do so are generally the type of people who have low EQ themselves and so can't recognize or pull off such subtleties. For those with solid EQ, it is hard to imagine life without soft skills, which are essential for successful IT Business Partners.

Chapter Fifteen

Selling IT Internally

Why is the concept of selling IT internally important to both you and your organization? Simply stated, the better IT performs, the more bottom-line results are delivered, and the more confidence your company will have in you. Promoting the business results driven through business technology convergence creates a positive feedback loop that increases opportunities for IT to continue adding to the bottom line. Yet some will say promoting IT successes too overtly is bragging and over the top. In truth, I'm not really advocating selling or promoting IT, per se. Instead of selling IT internally, consider it as strategically updating the organization about their IT investments. There isn't a CFO or sales team that doesn't look at progress against profit and revenue goals. And who doesn't celebrate when their company makes extra money or wins a big account? Communicating successes driven by IT is essentially the same thing. Still, some finesse can be a good thing when promoting IT-driven results.

IT Business Partners are well positioned to take the lead on communicating successes. They are closest to the solution, its benefits, and the impact on the organization and its customers. Sharing new capabilities is also a key deliverable of the release-planning efforts as outlined in chapter ten, and can be handled in numerous ways:

1. Business Technology Investment Committees
2. The Company Intranet & PMO
3. The Project Condition (PROCON) Model
4. IT Annual Reports

Idea One: Business Technology Investment Sessions

Chapter seven touched on the importance of helping end users understand how to request projects. When they do, they are more likely to be engaged in the process and get their ideas vetted and reviewed in the governance process. Equally important, end users who understand the decisions coming from the process tend to trust IT more. When projects are approved and then completed, IT governance sessions are an ideal forum to share successes. Make sharing completed projects a standing part of monthly governance meetings. IT Business Partners should lead this portion of the conversation. Invite end users as well, especially when the business results significantly improve operations or customer service. Include a slide or two to show each successful implementation since the last meeting. Where possible, include comments from end users or customers to demonstrate credibility. Allow attendees to ask questions. Consider including screenshots of new capabilities, or if warranted, perform a quick demo of a new solution.

VALUE DELIVERED

As you outline each success, be sure to remind attendees what the delivered value is and when you expect the benefits to be realized. By doing this each month, you remind your executives that the IT organization is hard at work doing the company's business. Executives are busy and you can't expect them to remember all the projects that are on IT's plate. Reviewing completed projects each meeting is a subtle but effective way to share successes without coming across as a political campaigner selling an idea.

VALUE-DELIVERED EXAMPLES

I have two simple examples of how you might consider sharing project successes. The first is an example of a project that resulted in an aging technology upgrade. Typically, this isn't the kind of thing that management teams get too excited about. They aren't exposed to it every day, and in this case the solution didn't directly impact revenue or touch customers. But by eliminating aging hardware and software, we were able to eliminate manufacturing risk and make operational improvements in reporting and efficiencies. The team that performed the work had to do much of it off-hours and on weekends when the company's manufacturing operations were typically offline.

In this example, we shared a few key messages. First, that the project team was so dedicated that they gave up evening and weekend family time to get the project done. Second, the team improved reporting and metrics for key operating platforms, advancing our quest to make operations more efficient. And third, we eliminated a manufacturing risk that had been in existence for a long time. If the older platform had crashed, which was becoming ever more likely, it would have stopped production, thus negatively impacting customer deliveries and resulting in lost revenue.

The IT Business Partner for this team accompanied the core project team on the implementations both as a show of support and to ensure that the platform was implemented as planned. This IT Business Partner was able to see firsthand how the project unfolded and the impact the solution had in our operations. Then, instead of leaving the accomplishments unsung as usual, we brought them to light by enumerating them, albeit briefly, at the BTIC IT governance session. IT gave upper management a few points to feel good about and in the process, subtly reinforced the general idea of IT's competence. The graphic we used to drive this message home was as simple as the slide presented below.

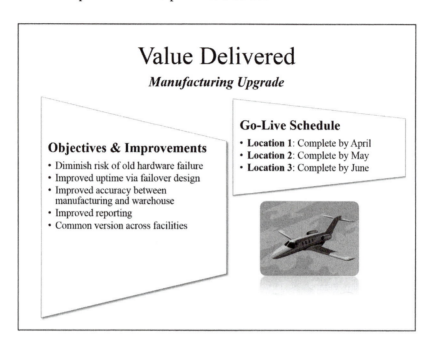

The second example centers on the implementation of a new Automatic Call Distribution System for our customer service team. We had a little fun with the project team and included a photo of their old phones with a "For Sale" sign stuck on them. In this case, the IT Business Partner talked about the value of being able to see call volumes, wait times, and abandoned calls, all in real time. In addition, he was able to show how the new solution would make this group more efficient, while at the same time enabling them to handle more customer calls. The IT Business Partner also discussed the future benefits of being able to analyze call data and to drive results proactively back to the sales and product teams. All of this was based on the data we were able to collect in the new system.

Again, rather than leave the impacts of the new technology unsung, the IT Business Partners acted as IT's advocate, highlighting the benefits and making it easy for management to see and appreciate the impact of the new technology. Here is what we presented to management to visually encapsulate and promote IT's success:

Value Delivered

Automated Call Distribution System

Benefits Summary
- Improved Customer Analytics
- Smoother Workload
- New Customer Insights
- Improved Business Continuity
- More Reliable Equipment
- Happier Customers & Customer Service Team Members

Used Phones for Sale!

These examples are simple but powerful. Even the most routine implementations can be exciting enough to share with executives when the business value of a new solution is well communicated. Make sure to add a value-delivered agenda item to the monthly governance meetings. Don't pass up an opportunity to show management how their investments are paying off.

Idea Two: Your Company Intranet and the PMO

Your company Intranet is an excellent resource to showcase business technology projects. I have long been a strong advocate for IT transparency. That includes sharing the results of the BTIC meetings, including which projects get funded and which don't. Employees expressing an interest in knowing what is being worked on have ready access when all active IT projects are detailed on your Intranet.

IT Business Partners should collaborate with the PMO to establish a platform where anyone in the company can see the status of a project, the open issues, upcoming milestones, and more. This transparency builds trust around the company and is an easy way to make IT accessible, yet many organizations fail to take advantage of it. Sharing the good, the bad, and the ugly of projects conveys that IT is open and trustworthy. It also dispels the notion that the inner-workings of the IT world are a dark chest of secrets, and instead promotes an aura of familiarity and accessibility, ultimately moving the needle toward business technology convergence.

PROJECT TRANSPARENCY IS CRUCIAL

Sharing project information can be a scary proposition. After all, projects are comprised of a series of (educated) guesses, from the first decision to pursue them all the way through final implementation. Invariably there are glitches with almost every project. The beauty of transparency is that when you display the complexity of project roadmaps, requirements, quality assurance, training, and everything else that goes into making a project successful, everyone can see the ups and downs of projects as they progress. In the non-transparent model, where business leaders are shielded from project complexities, IT successes are not advertised, and so management tends to only see the problems.

When executive management gets behind transparency, good things happen. People become more trusting, more open, and more honest about real issues facing the company. IT can lay that foundation by making business technology investments transparently available to everyone in the company.

For many years I worked with IT Business Partners, PMO directors, and company leaders to find good transparency solutions. Sharing details about active projects is something every organization should make a point to do. I always make sure that the company Intranet includes a project news section, project dashboards, and full project detail pages (sites) where employees can access everything about a project. We even decided to have some fun with it and named the site PNN (Project News Network) based on a well-known cable news outlet.

THE PNN LANDING PAGE

On PNN, our landing page was designed around news. We asked IT Business Partners and project managers to publish short news bulletins, updates, or just comments on a project. Sometimes IT Business Partners and project managers feel their plates are full enough with other, more important activities, and consequently they neglect the news section of PNN. But if the news site becomes stale, people will stop visiting it.

Alternatively, if you have a PMO administrative function, you might consider tasking them with the responsibility of posting updates to the news site. Another option is to post the results of the monthly BTIC meetings. We include a short note about any key decisions made by the committee and provide a link to that session's presentation so employees can see the same content as the executive team. This is what our PNN landing page looks like:

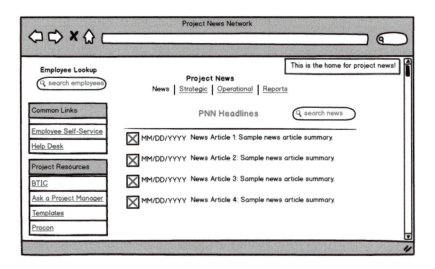

THE PNN PROJECT DASHBOARD

In addition to the landing page, we included two more project-based resources. The first is a project dashboard. Here employees can see a quick snapshot of all the active projects. We categorized them into three groups: strategic projects, operational projects, and reporting projects. Clicking on the links gives a quick view of the active projects in one of the three categories. Here is a look at our PNN project dashboard:

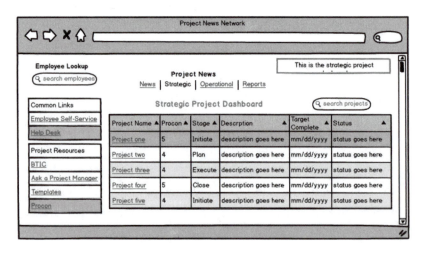

THE PNN PROJECT SITE

Project sites are the third leg of our transparency stool. Employees access the project sites by clicking on the link from the dashboard. On the project site, employees can see the latest status reports, project milestones, open issues, and any other project artifacts. Nothing is off-limits. Employees generally spend the vast majority of their time on the project dashboards. In contrast, the PMO staff, IT Business Partners, and project team members spend much of their time on the project sites. As you can see from the level of detail shown below, this is where their working documents were kept.

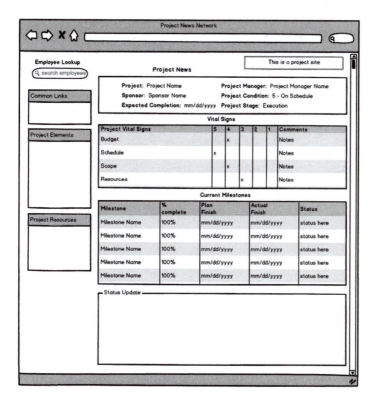

We had a bit of fun with PNN's announcement. In keeping with the news theme, we created a mock press release and distributed it to all employees via an email link; we also placed it as a lead story on our company's Intranet.

SAMPLE PNN PRESS RELEASE

Any Town, USA, September 09, 2012 – We are pleased to announce **Project News Network (PNN)**, a new Intranet site that is your source for project news and information. If you have ever wondered about the projects we are working on, then PNN is for you. The site provides access to our active project workload. You will also find articles and announcements meant to be interesting and informative. Below is a brief summary of what you will find inside PNN.

PNN's HOME PAGE

The home page has articles by members of our Project Management Office, IT Business Partners, and project team members. Here you will find behind-the-scene stories, information about vendors, links to our active project dashboards, and much more. You will also have quick access to FAQs, project templates, and how-to documents.

PNN PROJECT DASHBOARDS

Our project dashboards give a quick glimpse of the key projects underway. You will see the major investments that the company has chosen to undertake on the Strategic Project Dashboard. We have a number of shorter-term projects that are visible on the Operation Projects Dashboard. Finally, there is a snapshot of the key reporting and information projects on the Reporting Projects Dashboard.

Each view provides you with a short description of the project, the sponsor, key dates, and a brief update on project status.

THE PNN PROJECT SITES

If you have an appetite for more, the PNN Project Sites are for you. On project sites, you'll find the project team members' names, the current project charters and status reports, a list of open issues, and a calendar of key project milestones. If you are eager for even more, you can explore all of the working documents project teams use during the course of a project. This includes requirements documents, workflows, PowerPoint presentations, technical specs, and more.

Please take time to check out PNN, your source for project news. It will only take a few minutes to get familiar with the wealth of information available to you. Don't hesitate to contact us with any questions or suggestions.

Idea Three: The Project Condition (PROCON) Model

While working for the Bank of New York, our leadership team was working on launching a new Project Management Office. We were designing a project dashboard and we wanted a quick way to show the overall status of a project using something better than just the typical stoplight approach (where green means good, yellow means not as good, and red means trouble). Projects were too often green, even when they were experiencing hiccups along the way. I also had the sense that project managers used their gut feeling to score the status of their projects instead of real facts. I wanted a more rigorous tool that included guardrails around status and action steps for each status level. We knew that whatever we designed had to be easy for executives and sponsors to understand.

We had some movie buffs on the team who suggested an idea from the classic '80s Hollywood action thriller *War Games*. The movie was about a military computer that simulated war games, blurring the lines of reality and nearly causing World War III. The high-anxiety thriller shed light on the military's DEFCON (defense condition) status scale, which shows the overall state of military readiness at a glance. The five-scale system seemed like an effective solution to our problem. We especially liked that it showed subtle variations in the status of a project without sending the wrong signal to management. We also liked the rigor associated with each status level. Communication and action steps were outlined and triggered as the status changed from level to level.

We adapted the concept and changed the name to PROCON (project condition). I've used the five-scale system in PMOs at every company I have worked with since the Bank of New York, and have shared the idea with other PMO directors and IT leaders over the years. Most appreciate the status granularity and the rigor around communication and action steps when status levels change.

PROCON Scale

PROCON Scale

5	*All is well; full steam ahead*
4	*Minor setbacks, but manageable*
3	*Hitting some bumps; adjusting plans*
2	*Trouble ahead; need help*
1	*Red alert! Action required!*

PROCON Color Scale:
5-Dark Green,
4-Light Green,
3-Yellow,
2-Light Red,
1-Dark Red

© CIO Mentor, LLC – PROCON Levels

PROJECT HEALTH AT A GLANCE

In the PNN examples above, employees can surmise the health status of a project at a glance. Like DEFCON, our scale ranged from 5 (good status) to 1 (project derailed). It provides a clear and less subjective way to convey the status of the project. Management teams and sponsors warm to the five-scale system quickly. I have even seen non-IT project managers adapt the methodology for their business projects.

You might be wondering why this matters to IT Business Partners. The answer is that the PROCON is the primary way most executives keep tabs on a project. They don't usually read status reports or go in deep and review open issues. When they see the status of a project move from 5 to 4 or 4 to 3, they are more apt to ask why. Projects generally don't move from 5 to 3 in one fell swoop. It happens over time, task by task, milestone by milestone.

The five-scale system brings greater transparency to projects and contributes to the trust between IT and the business units. Executives and employees appreciate knowing that there is a quantifiable reason for each status level or change in level, and they have confidence in the ranking because they know there are defined actions associated with each level. The concept of PROCON has evolved at each company I've worked for. Ideas from business units and PMOs over the years have made the concept easier for executives to understand and easier for project managers to leverage. Below are two views of the PROCON model. One is designed for general audiences, and the other, more detailed, model is meant for the PMO.

General Audience PROCON Model

PROCON	Meaning	Key Steps	Assignment Criteria
5	All Is Well	• Smooth sailing! Full steam ahead!	• Schedule: On/ahead of schedule • Budget: At/under approved budget • Scope: No imact • Resources: No impact
4	Minor Setbacks, But Manageable	• Identify & communicate the impact in project status reports • Inform Project Sponsor & PMO	• Schedule: Within 10% or 4 weeks of plan • Budget: Within 10% or $50k over • Scope: Minor shifts: no key milestone impacts • Resources: Schedule variance within tolerance
3	Hitting Some Bumps, Adjusting Plans	• Project Sponsor, CIO & Director PMO notified • Plan to get back on track in 2 weeks • Prepare change requests • Finance involved for budget change requests	• Schedule: 10% or more than 1 month behind plan • Budget: 10% or more than $75k over • Scope: Key milestones at risk • Resources: Requires more staff to get back on schedule
2	Trouble Ahead; Help Needed	• Schedule regular meetings with PMO Director & Executive Sponsor • Keep CIO informed until we're out of the woods • Figure out how to get back on track within 4 weeks & prepare change requests as needed	• Schedule: 20% or more than 2 months behind plan • Budget: 20% or more than $100k over approved budget • Scope: Key milestones will be missed • Resources: Requires more resources to recover time on current schedule
1	Red Alert! Action Required	• Immediate review of project by Executive Sponsor, PMO Director & CIO • Finance revaluates business case • Project viability reassessed	• Schedule: Not possible to achieve plan • Budget: 25% or more than $150k over approved budget • Scope: All milestones at risk • Resources: No further work possible

© 2012 CIO Mentor, LLC

PMO PROCON Cheat Sheet					
PROCON		Schedule	Budget	Scope	Resources
ON TRACK	5	At/Ahead of schedule	Actual spend + ETC is at or under budget	No changes to requirements or deliverables	IT, business & vendor resources/ expertise are available to project.
UNDER CONTROL	4	Within 10% or 4 weeks	Actual spend + ETC variance within 10% or up to $50k	Some shifts in requirements or scope. Impact is within 10% or 4 weeks/$50k.	Resource shifts can be made. Schedule variance stays within 10% or 4 weeks.
Escalate & Communicate — Initiate Change Requests — BUMPY	3	Over 10% or 1 month	Actual spend + ETC variance 10% or $75k over	Changes to requirements/ deliverables negatively impacts budget or schedule.	Resources required for critical path tasks not available. Work can continue on other tasks.
TROUBLE AHEAD	2	Over 20% or 2 months	Actual spend + ETC variance 20% or $100k over	Requirement/ Deliverables differ materially from original charter.	Resources required for critical path tasks are not available with no alternatives.
IMMINENT FAILURE	1	Achievable schedule cannot be developed at this time.	Actual spend + ETC variance 25% over or $150k over (large projects)	Scope changes require complete review of approach and re-planning of budget, tasks & schedule.	Project at complete standstill due to resource unavailability.

© 2012 CIO Mentor, LLC

Idea Four: IT Annual Reports

I once worked for a major accounting firm whose offices were in a multi-tenant facility. Riding the elevator one day, I met a friendly individual from the company Intel. Their offices were on the floor just above ours. I'll call this woman Pat. She and I saw each other every day and mostly shared conversation about the weather and sports. One day, though, we ventured beyond idle chitchat and into a discussion about our jobs and interests.

We decided to meet and learn more about each other's business challenges and goals.

It was in our first meeting that I learned about Intel's knowledge-sharing practices and their commitment to the IT community. Pat shared a copy of their now-famous IT Annual Report. She explained that this excellent tool not only spreads information to the business units about the specific investment projects IT is working on, but also boosts IT morale by publicly acknowledging IT's contributions to the business overall. I was intrigued by the notion of producing an IT annual report for our organization. I shared the idea with my IT leadership team, and we decided to give it a try. We had just finished our "Day in the Life" strategy and felt that an IT annual report would communicate the success of that program while at the same time introducing IT to the entire organization. We had offices in over 100 cities, so meeting the IT organization in person wasn't practical for our more than 8,000 employees.

YOU DON'T HAVE TO SPEND A LOT

We didn't have Intel's IT budget, but we were confident we could still produce a meaningful report. We carved up assignments and launched our initiative. Here is how we structured our resulting 31-page IT annual report:

Elements	Contents
Cover Page	• A photo of a key end user, surrounded by IT staff members
Inside Cover	• A message about how we leveraged business technology innovation to help drive company strategy • The table of contents
Page 3 Welcome Message	• Welcome message from the CIO and a note on why we produced the annual report, what they could expect to find in the report, and an invitation to provide feedback
Pages 4 – 11 Meet Our Team	• An overview of each team (e.g., operations, collaborative systems, application development, Information Risk Management, and the PMO) • We included pictures of the leaders of each group and relevant statistics about our operation

Elements	Contents
Page 12 Organizing for Results	• Messaging relating to the power of IT & Business convergence • An overview of strategic vendor partners • A note about IT Governance and its importance
Page 14 User Experience Design	• Messaging relating to how we work • Emphasis on being in the field and working side-by-side with audit & tax teams
Pages 15 – 28 Balanced Scorecard & Value Delivered	• Highlights of key accomplishments in four areas (Financial, Customer, Operations, and Learning) • Accomplishments including key results metrics • Timeline & key deliverables for the past few years across the bottom of all pages in this section
Pages 29 – 31 Key Messages and a Look Ahead	• Messaging around continuing our partnership. Included an overview of the road ahead for the upcoming year by business unit. • A full-page graphic of our "Day in the Life" cartoon

The notion of selling IT accomplishments is often perceived by IT professionals as over the top or gratuitous. It may feel that way at first, but leveraging the tools outlined in this chapter underscores the legitimate value that IT partnerships bring to an organization. Unfortunately, you will always have people who assume the worst intentions. That happened at the accounting firm when we produced our annual report. We had a few partners express frustration that we would even take the time to prepare such a report. They assumed we spent a ton of time and thousands of dollars getting the report printed. We actually used a printing company that was a customer of the firm. We printed a few thousand reports for an upcoming partners' meeting at a cost of under $5,000, which was easily absorbed in our budget, and made the report available as a PDF on our Intranet. We did the project in our spare time. We took candid photos of the IT organization during meetings, and each of my direct reports produced articles and overviews for each of their departments. It took just a few months to assemble the whole package, and in the end, it consumed very little of our time.

We did all of the editing and formatting ourselves. The advance of self-publishing tools made this simple to do on our own.

Once our partners realized this, the overwhelming response from our executive team was positive. I received numerous favorable comments from around the firm. The vast majority of them thanked us for the transparency and offered content suggestions for next year's report. The response was well worth the effort. I heard from a number of executives that the annual report really made a positive impression on them and helped them to better understand the contributions of the IT organization. We made sure to get a copy on every IT staff member's desk the day they came back from the printer. The response from them was also overwhelmingly positive. It helped boost morale. People told me that they felt proud to be a part of our team. It created buzz and a positive glow for many months after publishing.

Summary: Deliver Value

All four of the techniques outlined in this chapter will need to be tailored to your organization's culture and style to ensure they deliver the best possible impact. However you do it, IT must make it a priority to proactively communicate the status of IT projects and initiatives to the organization. It is tempting to put this off and focus on the work at hand. But neglecting to promote and communicate IT's project portfolio and successes just isn't an option if you want the partnership program and the IT organization to be recognized as the valued asset it is. Here is a short summary of the tools and concepts outlined in this chapter:

→ **BTIC:** Highlights the value delivered and reviews project progress each month. This is essential to keeping executives engaged and up-to-date on how the company's business technology investments are faring.

→ *PNN:* Communicates full transparency to the entire organization via the Intranet and invokes trust and confidence.

→ *PROCON:* Leverages a simple color-coded status model to indicate the overall health of projects and communicates the message that IT is in control and can be counted on.

→ ***Annual Report:*** Introduces the IT team and Business Partnership program to the entire organization and is a simple way to show the impact IT has in achieving strategic company goals and objectives.

Chapter Sixteen

Connecting and Networking

The moment someone becomes an IT Business Partner, they stop working by themselves and begin working collaboratively with others. Thus, the value of networking cannot be overstated. IT Business Partners never know when they are going to meet someone who has an idea that solves a problem or provides insight into a challenge. Inspiration comes from many sources: a chance meeting in an elevator, a networking breakfast, a seminar, a phone call with a vendor. For me, the idea of networking is not an option; it is a critical part of my job.

IT Business Partners should make it a priority to network inside as well as outside the company. They should include vendors in their network activities as well. Ideas come from many unexpected sources. One of the strengths IT Business Partners have is their ability to connect the dots between seemingly disparate situations and events. Think of networking as an activity that provides multiple discreet data points of intellectual fodder that will come together in amazing and impactful ways. IT Business Partners who take this view can look forward to networking opportunities, instead of considering them an onerous social obligation. To stay on top of their game, IT Business Partners have to keep the supply of fresh exposures and new information streaming in.

Formalize Your Networking Program

Consider thinking formally about how IT Business Partners approach networking. Make it more than a casual happenstance. Encourage them to include social media, face-to-face meetings, seminars, industry conferences, and local professional organizations as part of their overall networking program. Suggest that they consider their network as a personal supply chain of ideas and solutions. Otherwise they are essentially taking the world on by themselves. This is the antithesis of everything IT Business Partners stand for. Remind them that they do not have to be an extrovert to be good at networking. The ideas below will help them get started.

Leverage Social Media

→ *LinkedIn:* If you don't have a LinkedIn account, get one soon. If you already have one, make sure it is up-to-date. Review your profiles and work history regularly. This will help you as you make connections with others on the site. Take a look at the news feeds periodically. People enjoy sharing what they are working on and are usually happy to share their ideas. Explore LinkedIn professional groups that you could join. In these groups, owners pose questions to engage members, making this an excellent way to network and a great source of new ideas.

→ *Twitter:* Establish a Twitter account. Find industry experts to follow. These experts often share ideas and articles that IT Business Partners will find helpful. Tweet occasionally and judiciously, being careful not to give away company secrets or inside information. Follow tweets from competitors. There is always something to learn from what they have to say.

→ *Blogs:* Consider both following industry blogs and starting your own. Writing is a great way to hone your communication skills and solicit feedback on ideas or problems you might be dealing with. When you make the effort to share first, people are more apt to share their ideas in return.

Join Professional Organizations

→ *PDMA:* Join a local chapter of the Product Development Management Association. If your city doesn't have a chapter, consider starting one. Product managers are a great resource for IT Business Partners.

→ *PMI:* Consider joining the Project Management Institute. While there isn't a direct link to the IT Business Partner role, you can learn how other companies handle their intake and Business Case development processes.

→ *Local Professional Organizations:* Many local consulting organizations form networking groups as a way to bring like-minded people together. Work with a respected local firm and start an IT Business Partner forum. If that isn't possible, see if there are other groups that might be worth joining. A local firm that I worked with in the Twin Cities has taken networking up a notch. They carved out a non-vendor-sponsored function and invited CIOs, IT leaders, CFOs, and many others to join specific groups. They established social media sites and a website where members can network and share ideas with no vendor involvement. Try to find something similar in your area.

Attend Industry Conferences

→ *Industry Conferences:* Make sure IT Business Partners attend industry conferences as time and budget allow. This is a great way to meet new people, hear about the challenges other organizations face, and learn about their approaches to dealing with them.

For example, each year I make it a point to attend the Internet Retailer Conference and the Gartner Symposium to network and learn from others.

→ **Vendor Conferences:** Attending key vendor conferences is another way to see how others are solving everyday problems in business. Cloud vendors, ERP vendors, and many others offer great networking opportunities.

Capitalize on Personal Networking Opportunities

→ **Friday Networking:** I try and reserve a part of each Friday for networking so that I am meeting with one or two people each workweek to exchange ideas. As word gets around that this is a regular thing, requests to meet tend to increase. This kind of networking is invaluable to me in my job. Sharing ideas and experiences in a relaxed forum at a local coffee shop is not a bad way to fuel thinking. Be warned that sometimes you will wake up on a Friday morning and think, "I don't feel like networking today." Fight the urge, get out there, and do it anyway. You will be surprised by the energy and ideas that networking delivers. I am rarely disappointed.

→ **Public Speaking:** Look for opportunities to speak publically. Present the company's approaches to field research, investment roadmaps, or strategic plans. Preparing presentations challenges you to hone your message and approach, making you a more clear and succinct Business Partner.

Summary: Stay Connected

The benefits of networking have long been an important and essential tool for professional development. Building and then nurturing a professional network provides access to ideas and people that can help IT Business Partners along the way. Networking can also lead to career opportunities and help you find needed staff, learn about vendors, and hear firsthand about industry trends. In short, it is the best way to maintain an inventory of fresh and relevant ideas. Take time to plan an IT Business Partner networking strategy. Don't leave it up to chance, and don't put it on the back burner. The benefits of networking cannot be overstated.

Chapter Seventeen

Hype and the Marketplace

The pace of marketplace change is more rapid now than in any time in history. Companies don't often stay on top of their industries in the same way they did years ago. Just look at the cell phone industry. Motorola started the craze in the '80s, the market shifted to Nokia in the '90s, then to RIM's BlackBerry. Apple's iPhone rode the wave for eighteen months, and then Samsung overtook Apple. There are more upstarts that reach market prominence than ever before. Companies like Facebook and Google seem to have come out of nowhere to reach market prominence in the blink of an eye.

Hyper-Changing Markets

The hyper-changing marketplace puts pressure on organizations to adapt in order to remain competitive. Many business leaders say adaptability has emerged as a required core competency for companies. IT Business Partners have a front-row seat to fast-paced change, and they need to take advantage of it. You will most certainly face hyper-change challenges as you develop Capability Roadmaps and Release Plans for your business units. You will have to contend with vendors selling directly to end users in an attempt to cut IT out of the loop. You will face new-solution deployment challenges as more companies adapt a bring-your-own-device model. In addition, the wave of new smartphones and tablets is changing how companies go to market. IT Business Partnership success will be measured in part by how well you anticipate and take advantage of the challenges born of increasingly rapid change.

WHEN WILL IT END?

When will the pace of change slow or stop? Never! That is the nature of markets. As long as there is a free-enterprise system, there will always be new innovations coming from new technologies and competitors. The good news is that the fundamentals of field research will help you and your IT Business Partners see where plans should be adjusted. Putting the customer first has long been a mantra of many organizations. Given the ever increasing pace of change, this approach couldn't be more critical.

IT Business Partners have a large role to play ensuring that the company and business units do not grow too inwardly focused. This is easy for companies to do, especially when times get tough and the attention turns to cost savings and efficiency initiatives. Take care to preserve a balance between inward and outward focus by keeping on top of field research; otherwise you run the risk of being left in the dust by the fast pace of change.

Journey Mapping

An emerging business process skill called Customer Journey Mapping has taken on more prominence in recent years. Forrester Research, Gartner, and Harvard Business Review have all written extensively about the benefits of Journey Mapping. Forrester now publishes a Customer Experience Index annually where they measure the state of customer experiences in more than 160 companies.

Interest in Journey Mapping is on the rise as more companies see the power, insight, and promise it delivers. In response to this demand, more consulting firms are emerging that specialize in this practice. Some say we are now in an age where customers are driving companies to make products available in ways that best serve them. IT Business Partners that master Journey Mapping will be ahead of the curve in understanding customers and driving value for their company.

What is a Customer Journey Map? Journey Maps capture a visual representation of customer touch points. They highlight customer perceptions and needs over the course of a customer's relationship with your company. Since one of the contributions of an IT Business Partner is to keep the company informed of in-the-field customer experiences, Journey Maps are an excellent tool to utilize, and can be used to develop a deeper understanding of what customers see and feel during their interactions with your company. They can also be leveraged to develop internal and external training and communication programs. Below is a summary of the key elements of a Journey Map:

Elements of a Customer Journey Map	
Customer interaction chronology	**Pain points**, gaps, and disconnects in service
Goals and needs at each process step	**Brand impact**, satisfaction, and emotional responses
Moments of truth (impact areas) in the overall customer experience	**Business process touch points** including roles, systems, and provider departments
Improvement opportunities for existing services	

THE IMPLICATIONS OF NOT UNDERSTANDING THE JOURNEY

There is a scenario faced by every consumer goods manufacturer when they make the decision to sell directly to consumers online. Direct-selling channels create channel conflict for retailers and consumer goods distributers. Prior to digital channels, consumer goods manufacturers didn't have to worry about channel conflict. Now that direct selling online is commonplace, retailers and distributors are understandably concerned about how e-commerce and mobile capabilities affect them. Their core fear is being cut out of customer sales.

Leverage the principles of Journey Mapping to gain insight into how distributors and retailers are impacted by this change. Journey Mapping unveils the retailer and distributor touch points with your company. The mapping process enables you to put yourself in their minds. When you do, it doesn't take long to see the moments of truth and the adverse impact to your brand if solutions aren't designed to keep retail partners whole. In fact, be sure to look at consumers the same way. Correlate their experience with your retailers and distributors. In doing so, you will be equipped to head off frustrated customers and retailers and the negative impact on your company's brand overall.

Take this simple consumer-buying example: A customer shops online, buys a product, and asks for home delivery. Upon arrival, the customer realizes that the product doesn't fit. Their option is a return via FedEx or to bring the product back to a store.

Imagine you are the store owner in this scenario. The customer purchased and paid for the product online. As the store owner you didn't receive any revenue from the sale. What incentive would you have to service this customer? You may be inclined to discourage the customer from returning the product to your store, thereby confusing and frustrating them. The results would have a detrimental impact on the company brand and reduce the likelihood of the customer becoming a repeat buyer.

Journey Mapping reveals the processes and solutions that need changing to preserve customers, your retailers, and ultimately, your company's brand. Armed with a clearer picture of the critical pain points, you will be better able to develop business processes and solutions that do just that. To garner support for the proposed changes, take the ideas to your retailers while they are still on paper and let them weigh in on the process before the ideas are finalized. This simple act secures their confidence in your company, and ensures that your end-customers will enjoy the best possible experience with retailers, regardless of how they initiated a transaction.

Sometimes the touch points on the customer journey are a little less obvious. While working for a consumer goods manufacturer, many of our customers didn't know we had a full repair shop. Our cobblers repaired shoes from the ground up and made them look brand-new. Our marketing team decided to promote the repair service and launched a general awareness campaign with a video highlighting our capabilities. We announced the new video on all of our social media sites, and the positive responses were off the charts. The video was an instant hit, showcasing all that was good about our company.

Good news for us! Except for one thing: we didn't think to give the shoe repair team a heads-up. The response to the video was so overwhelming that our customers sent in shoes for repair in numbers we had never seen. The repair shop was swamped without warning, resulting in a huge service backlog. Fortunately, we were able to add enough staff to keep up with the pace of demand, and the customer impacts were only short-term.

Had we thought about the customer's journey a bit more in this case, I am confident that we would have anticipated the increased volume and we could have proactively added more staff members. In other words, we would have officially uncovered an issue in advance and then designed a business process solution to solve the problem. This would have meant less scrambling for us internally, but even more importantly, it would have preserved the integrity of our customers' experience with us and protected our overall brand image.

Journey Mapping is an effective method for IT Business Partners to keep pace with customers and shape strategic plans. The more IT Business Partners know about the customers and their experiences with the company, the more they can deliver solutions that hit the mark strategically.

Cloud Computing and IT Business Partners

A very real challenge for IT Business Partners and IT organizations in general relates to the explosion of cloud-based solutions. Many cloud vendors like Salesforce.com make it a practice to sell directly to business users, instead of the IT department, in an attempt to circumvent established IT project-vetting processes. These vendors can make the solutions they sell seem almost magical. They even offer a pay-as-you-go philosophy, making the decision processes so easy that any business unit with a credit card can be lured into launching a cloud-based service. At the same time, some cloud vendors want commitments to minimum user levels and annual maintenance fees in advance in an attempt to make it feel more like a traditional licensed software model. All is not as simple as it might seem in the cloud computing world.

Cloud computing puts significant pressure on organizations, especially those that don't have clear strategies and vision. IT Business Partners can mitigate these pressures. Like any other initiative, cloud computing solutions need to fit into your strategic framework. Only by having IT Business Partners who understand your company's vision and strategy can IT effectively map the appropriate solutions, cloud or otherwise, into your company's investment roadmap.

Some of the business parameters that IT Business Partners need to consider include:

→ *Business Requirements:* Cloud computing doesn't eliminate the need to define a company's business requirements. It is common for cloud newbies to assume that business requirements are already determined. But business requirements aren't magically sprinkled into cloud computing solutions. You still need to think about your unique business processes and requirements and then design the right solutions, regardless of whether the services come from your data center or the cloud.

→ *Business Integration:* Cloud solutions aren't usually stand-alone, and you need to consider if and how they should be integrated with other business applications. IT Business Partners will have to work with IT architects to best determine how everything should be integrated. The IT Business Partner's insight is instrumental in developing a plan that reduces the impact of what end users will see when switching from an in-house-provided solution to a cloud solution.

→ *Business Data:* This dovetails with the business integration concept above. You will need to leverage the business information in the cloud solution and use it in the reporting and information solutions. For example, there might be an information data warehouse with which the cloud data needs to integrate in order to ensure consistent reporting across all business applications.

→ *Capital versus Expense:* CFOs will care about this issue. With traditional in-house business applications, buying servers and related software to run email and ERP systems requires a capital outlay. Companies typically spread the costs of this capital (depreciation for server hardware and amortization for software) over a period of years. With cloud computing there isn't a capital outlay, and costs hit the bottom line immediately because it is a subscription service with a monthly fee typically based on the number of users. There might be other costs too, such as charges for the network connection between the cloud provider and the company's operations. IT Business Partners need to take this into account when building investment Business Cases.

→ ***Security & Compliance Considerations:*** This is often overlooked in the early stages of cloud computing. However, security and compliance matters are crucial points to consider when implementing cloud capabilities. Seemingly simple matters such as how users will sign in to the new application come into play: Will they use their current user ID and password, or are another set of IDs and passwords required? IT Business Partners consider these factors and help marshal the right resources to determine how security for cloud solutions will be handled in the organization.

Summary: Embrace Change

Marketplace change is occurring at a more rapid pace than at any time in history. Companies must become more flexible and adaptable to respond to the changing market conditions. To keep pace with all this constant change, it is critical for IT Business Partners to stay connected to customers and consumers. Many available tools facilitate this, including field research and Journey Mapping. Concurrently, the proliferation of cloud-based solutions is creating both opportunities and challenges for businesses. IT Business Partners need to embrace cloud solutions while at the same time keeping business requirements and secure access in mind.

Afterword

Few roles afford the opportunity to see your company and its customers in the intimate way the role of IT Business Partner does. As they move your company toward business technology convergence, IT Business Partners witness firsthand customer interactions with your company's products and services. They work with business units as they drive strategic plans. They bring new ideas to the table that respond to market and operational priorities. And, they see how internal operational functions within the company work together to provide the best possible products and services to a customer. What other role has the potential to connect to customers, business units, the supply chain, finance, IT, marketing, and HR?

An IT Business Partner is a business person first. They must understand how the company makes money, what motivates customers, how operations work, and how the IT organization connects the dots between all those entities. They are also a strategist. They have to understand each business unit's challenges and each customer's challenges, and bring them together as part of a strategic plan with clearly defined key service offerings and operational capabilities.

They are even a salesperson. IT Business Partners have to be able to package their ideas in a way that highlights pain points, solutions, and new operating realities to gain executive support and win finance dollars. Then they have to judiciously advertise IT department accomplishments effectively enough to ensure funding for future strategic IT initiatives. Successful IT Business Partners need to spend time communicating initiatives, successes, and the bottom-line business results to all levels of the company. This includes Capability Roadmaps, Release Plans, Business Cases, and more. In some respects, IT Business Partners are marketing communication specialists, too. Helping business units and employees understand the realities of the intake process for projects and the constraints of budgets takes skill and patience.

And finally, yes, IT Business Partners are IT professionals. They know how to leverage the power of IT and how to unleash its potential to solve the company's needs and those of the individual business units. Effective IT Business Partnership programs move organizations beyond simple alignment toward a model where IT is leveraged strategically and true business technology convergence is achieved. Organizations that achieve this convergence will significantly outperform their competitors and deliver bottom-line results that are hard to argue with.

The process begins by defining an IT Business Partnership role uniquely suited to your company so that it can be well understood. You will have many options to consider as you outline how your partners will align to business units. Collaboration and communication with business unit leaders will help you develop a program that has the correct foundation and support right from the start.

Once you have the structure mapped out, concentrate on finding the right resources. You will need to find candidates with the right blend of strategic, relationship building, communication, and creative skills to make the role credible and meaningful in your organization. Developing a formal career path for IT Business Partners helps send a message that the role is just like any other officially structured management role in your organization. It can then fit into the compensation framework like these other roles do and be recognized by management and your HR team as a vitally important role in your company.

I hope that this book gives you a clear idea of what an IT Business Partnership program should look like and the value it can bring to your company. I also hope that it causes you to regard IT as an equally vital business unit, as are all the other business units, and that it gives you the language and confidence to convey this message to everyone in your organization.

Most of all, I hope that you can use this book as the subtitle suggests: as a guide to use in the field as you start your own IT Business Partnership program, and as a resource to refer to as your program develops.

I have met and worked with many great people along the way. Each of them has helped to shape and improve the concepts outlined in this book. I want to thank all of you who had the patience and loyalty to stick with the program over the years. Building IT Business Partnership programs isn't easy, but when done well, the results are an unending source of personal and financial reward.

Bibliography

BTM Institute. (2007). *Business Technology Convergence Index.* Stamford Connecticut: BTM Institute.

BTM Institute. (2009). *BTM Technology Convergence Index II.* Stamford, Connecticut: BTM Corporation.

Bussey, J. (2013, January 22). "A Transformative Time for Companies— and Their CIOs." *Wall Street Journal,* p. B11.

CIO Magazine. (2012). "2012 State of the CIO." Framingham, MA: CXO Media.

Forrester, Nigel Fenwick. (2011). *Beyond Alignment: A Road Map.* Boston, MA: Forrester Research.

Goleman, D. (1995). *Emotional Intelligence.* New York, NY: Bantam.

Heller, M. (2012). *The CIO Paradox.* Brookline, MA: Bibliomotion.

High, P. (2009). *World Class IT.* San Francisco, CA: Jossey-Bass.

Lencioni, P. (2002). *The Five Dysfunctions of a Team.* San Francisco, CA: Jossey-Bass.

Rath, T. (2007). *StrengthsFinder 2.0.* New York, NY: Gallup Press.

Turak, A. (2012, July 17). "The 11 Leadership Secrets You Never Heard About." *Forbes magazine.*

Weirsema, M. T. (1995). *The Discipline of Market Leaders.* New York, NY: Perseus Books.

Index